The Cranks Recipe Book is our response to the thousands of our customers who have consistently asked us for the 'know-how' of Cranks food. And now here are over 300 recipes which we are confident will bring the spirit of Cranks to you.

Kay Canter's own wholefood recipes from home began the treasury in the early days. Twenty-two years later it has been enriched by the passing touches of many caring Cranks cooks, finding recipes, testing recipes and making them work to perfection. Now this wide repertoire has been returned to the home scale. We know you will find they work, thanks to the efforts of Kay and the skills of delightful home economist Jane Suthering. Together they test-cooked in weekly sessions over eighteen months to satisfy our standards of taste and clear presentation. Some say we are crazy to give away our secrets to possible competitors! We hope you will enjoy trying them out in your own home.

David Canter

D0724598

DAVID CANTER · KAY CANTER
DAPHNE SWANN

THE
CRANKS
RECIPE
BOOK

Grafton

An Imprint of HarperCollins*Publishers*

Grafton
An Imprint of HarperCollins*Publishers*
77–85 Fulham Palace Road,
Hammersmith, London W6 8JB

Published by GraftonBooks 1985
Reprinted eighteen times
9 8 7 6

First published in Great Britain by
J. M. Dent & Sons Ltd 1982

Copyright © Cranks Ltd 1982

ISBN 0 586 06090 1

Set in Plantin

Printed in Great Britain by
HarperCollinsManufacturing Glasgow

Contents

TO DAVID

Who was the founder, inspiration and creative architect of Cranks.

David Canter died very suddenly on 1 July 1981. He dedicated many hours of work to the writing, production and design of this book, which was almost completed at his death. We have tried to keep the book as close as possible to the original text and offer it as a tribute to his memory.

Acknowledgments

Cranks would not have succeeded or possessed its special character without the contributions of many staff, suppliers and friends. We would like to thank them all, not only for their work on our behalf but for the little bit of themselves that has become part of the Cranks personality. In particular we would like to thank the following by name:

DAVID'S FATHER, Norman Canter, who lent us £500 for the first Cranks restaurant, and never asked for it back!

EDWARD BAWDEN, whose distinctive drawings ornamented our first brochure and are still used today.

DONALD JACKSON, whose calligraphy and graphics have contributed so much to the unmistakable style of Cranks.

JOHN LAWRENCE, the artist and illustrator, whose beautiful wood engravings adorn our literature.

RAY FINCH (and his team at Winchcombe), whose beautiful stoneware pottery has contributed so much to Cranks' image and who has consistently and relentlessly supplied us with literally thousands of cups, saucers, bowls, plates and so on over the years.

DAVID RANSOM, interior designer, who worked with David Canter on the design of Cranks restaurants and the Dartington Cider Press Centre.

JAMES AND SUE MORE-MOLYNEUX, of Loseley Park Farm, who started making yoghourt in 1969 and, together with their son Mike, make our dairy products to such a high standard.

SAM MAYALL, of Pimhill in Shropshire, whose farm is a paragon of organic husbandry.

MIRIAM POLUNIN, who with sensitive expertise assisted us in restructuring some of the text.

JANE SUTHERING, for her invaluable work on the recipes and text.

SHIRLEY-ANNE DOWTHWAITE, our wonderful secretary who has helped us in a thousand ways, in addition to the endless checking and typing of this book.

Our thanks to the countless others over the years who have worked for us; and, not least, our thanks to our current team and management.

The story of Cranks by David Canter

On our first day of business, 21 June 1961, we had no idea how much food to prepare. We had not advertised the opening of Cranks restaurant at 22 Carnaby Street, then a quiet backwater. So we were pleasantly suprised when a steady stream of people came in to fill our fifty seats. They saw a modest-sized ground floor and basement where every item of food and furnishing expressed the same values: simple natural materials used in a direct and craftsmanly way.

On the menu were mainly salads, of a completely different kind from what most of those new customers would have connected with the word. In contrast to the traditional tired lettuce that makes the appetite wilt too, these salads could change the eater's whole view of vegetables. The vivid combinations of ingredients and colours, crisp from fresh cutting and dressing, were teamed with equally fresh wholemeal rolls, soups, savouries and puddings. The quality of the materials used to make all these – only 100% wholemeal flour, raw Barbados sugar, free-range eggs, fresh fruit and dairy produce – was matched by the surroundings. Now familiar but then revolutionary to most people's eyes was the use of handthrown stoneware pottery, solid natural-coloured oak tables, heather brown quarry tiles, woven basket lampshades and hand-woven seat covers, among the white painted brick arches of the bakeshop we had toiled to convert with a borrowed £500.

Both food and surroundings have changed only in detail during all the expansion of the next twenty-one years. They already expressed the ideals of Cranks three owners and partners, who, with our first helper Netty, formed the entire staff that busy day.

As the restaurant flourished in spite of being tucked away,

we were delighted that so many other people wanted to seek out the experience we were offering, in what was a step into the unknown for the three of us.

Although a draughtsman by training, I had been running my family's pen shop business. Daphne Swann was a close friend and colleague there. My wife, Kay Canter, was busy looking after our three young children. So, as hundreds of visitors to Cranks have asked us, 'How did you begin?'

Although Kay, Daphne and I are equal partners, they agree that it was from me that the creation of Cranks came.

The first force at work was my great leaning towards sculpture, pottery and painting that even from school years made me want to be a designer. It was from my love of craftsmanship and natural materials that the style, which is unique to Cranks, was to come. Craftsmanship such as that of calligrapher Donald Jackson, for instance, who has lettered all our brochures and signs, raises what is so often a mundane means-to-an-end to an enriching level of beauty and creativity.

The second and more direct inspiration began with a slipped disc, in 1950. The complete failure of treatment requiring weeks of bed rest, hospital traction sessions, plaster jackets (with unreachable itches!) and strong pain-killing drugs left me very depressed.

At my father's suggestion, I went for treatment to a distinguished osteopath (Mr Puttock). He spent our sessions of back manipulation re-educating me about health, including giving me several books to read. One of them was Gaylord Hauser's *Look Younger, Live Longer*. The effect was dramatic – an exciting and fascinating reversal of all Kay's and my ideas of health and disease.

We had been brought face to face with the fact that I was individually responsible for my health and well-being, and that a major factor in how healthy I would be was what I ate.

We were completely convinced by the obvious sense of a philosophy which stresses that nature knows best, and so the food we eat should be as near as possible to the form in which it is harvested. Only then will it still have the complex blend of ingredients that still defies complete analysis, and yet is so essential to man's health and vitality.

We lost no time in putting our new-found knowledge into practice. We ceremoniously put all our white sugar, aspirins and other medicines down the lavatory and pulled the chain. We were determined that our three young children should not suffer the ills we had, but should be given the natural, unrefined foods that would build the good health that was their birthright.

In spite of this conviction, we might never have thought of adventuring into a restaurant if it had not been for Ronald Beesley of the College of Psychotherapeutics. Daphne had suggested he could help me with the depression after my back problem. He was an amazing man who seemed to have a link with a spiritual power beyond ordinary comprehension. He quickly revived the life force within me, and I developed a new approach to life that later made our venture much easier.

I now felt a certainty that once I had decided on a course of action springing from the right motivation, and provided I put aside fear and had confidence, even when the path was scattered with the most frightening obstacles, all would be overcome. Fear is the corrosive factor which has within it the seeds of failure.

In this frame of mind, when a vacant bakeshop came to our attention while I was converting similar premises into the first showroom of the Craftsman Potters Association in the same street, we did not hesitate. At that time, Carnaby Street was not swinging, but a street of small shops and cafés – a saddlery, a chess shop, an ironmongers, tailors and more. Rents were low.

Takings on our first day totalled £11. 17s. 1d; with such a brisk start we gladly took on Joe Doyle, a Sydney girl who came in to have a meal and then asked for a job. Joe was the first of the many wonderful staff who have worked for us – so many of whom were from Australia or New Zealand. They possessed the ideal spirit for working in Cranks by approaching the work with enthusiasm and down-to-earth commonsense. They also looked very attractive in the blue floral dresses that we have used as our uniform from the beginning.

Working at Cranks is different from the usual restaurant. Instead of the hierarchy of jobs, ours was the amateur, family-style approach. Our staff are members of a team working on first name terms with a sense of comradeship. We don't subscribe to 'the customer is always right' theory; we feel that staff and customers come together as equally as host and guest. We also avoid the use of 'sirs' or 'madams', and we don't accept the degrading habit of tipping.

Our staff have turned their hands to all the jobs – preparing, cooking, serving, cleaning up. So have we, creating over the years associations with many special characters among staff and suppliers, as problems have arisen and been solved. Nowadays, for instance, every Cranks has its own bakery. We went through many stages to achieve this from Kay baking at home, to our staff using a domestic oven in the Carnaby Street basement kitchen, to the final discovery that Sam Mayall's flour and Doris Grant's no-knead bread recipe was the perfect combination from which the famous Cranks loaf emerged – still unchanged for the last fifteen years. Today, we produce over 400 Cranks loaves and 550 cheese baps a day, in addition to all the cakes, pastries and savouries.

Vegetables grown organically, without synthetic chemicals, are as important to us in our principles as compost-grown wheat, though we have always found it extremely difficult to find sufficient regular suppliers. For twenty years, Graham has brought us fruit and vegetables faithfully day in, day out, from the old Covent Garden Market (now Nine Elms) to make up the shortage from organic sources.

Our urgent need for a reliable supply of natural and fresh fruit yoghourts led us to approach James More-Molyneux, whose ready response resulted in Loseley becoming one of the largest suppliers of additive-free yoghourt and ice-cream for the whole of the south of England.

By the mid-60s Carnaby Street had become so famous for its 'trendy' clothes stores that we have been featured as background in dozens of documentaries. We had established a rabbit warren of small, neighbouring premises giving us a Salad Bar, a Juice Bar, a health food store and a bakery, in addition to our over-crowded restaurant.

By now, we were 'bursting at the seams' and we leapt at the opportunity in 1967 to move into larger premises in nearby

Marshall Street with seating for 170 people and a large adjoining shop. This is now the Cranks home base, from where in the next decade we opened offshoots in Dartmouth, Totnes, Guildford and Dartington.

We weren't expanding out of London just for fun, although we have only opened in places where we have felt an affinity with the area. Country sites could be opened at a much lower cost, and the property freeholds provided security for bank loans which had to make up for our shortage of capital.

Many flattering overtures from individuals and international groups to open more Cranks or even Cranks franchises at home and overseas have been declined. We have wanted to remain a relatively small concern where we could maintain tight control of food and aesthetic standards. But when Heals of Tottenham Court Road, London, and the Peter Robinson group at Oxford Circus each invited us to open up Cranks restaurants which allowed us our own style and control, we did. The exception is the Cranks Grønne Buffet, opened in 1979 by Daniel and Yette Hage in Copenhagen. Because of the distance, our annual visit to them gives us a rare chance to sit together quietly and take a bird's eye view of everything we are doing at Cranks.

It has always been a basic principle of ours that each Cranks should be a self-sufficient unit. However small, it must have its own bakery to produce bread, savouries and cakes. This is not only to simplify organization and avoid delivery services but, more importantly, it gives each branch a sense of wholeness and job satisfaction, because the staff can be totally involved.

A problem that is constantly with us is how to pitch our prices and decide how much we can afford to pay in salaries. There are many people who think that because we own and run a business with a turnover of over £2 million a year we must be wealthy. This is far from the case!

We were lucky enough to receive some very sound basic advice from our accountants before we opened. They suggested we multiplied our food costs by three to arrive at the menu price and kept our salaries within 25% of takings (it is currently between 28 and 30%). We have stuck to this over the years, and those of our customers who may think our prices too high are, with the greatest respect, unaware of the specially high cost of our kind of operation.

Although they are right in thinking that our choice of buffet service requires fewer staff, far more are required behind the scenes than at most restaurants. Because we make every dish fresh daily from basic ingredients, there is a vast amount of washing, chopping and preparing that other restaurants avoid, often using ready-made mixes and pre-packed vegetables instead.

Our ingredients are also more expensive than the catering norm. A notable example is our use of free-range eggs only, when we could use powdered eggs from battery farms at a fraction of the price. The pleasure of eating from handthrown stoneware, in our view, outweighs the thousands of pounds spent a year replacing it. Our customers must like it – they have always tended to take some home with them!

Each partner has played a different role. Daphne has become a very effective businesswoman, responsible for the day-to-day affairs of purchasing, employing and control of staff, and many of the other facets in keeping Cranks running smoothly. One of Daphne's qualities has been her ability to be in sympathy with the staff, in a way that brings out the best in them and helps the team feeling. She can also get her teeth into a problem and see it through.

Kay has gradually been able to give more time to the business as our children have grown up. Her devotion to 'good housekeeping' – standards of food, cleanliness and service – is so strong as to be creative, not in any way secondary. It is Kay who keeps Cranks in touch with animal protection and anti-pollution societies, so that their leaflets and concerns come to the attention of thousands of our customers.

As to myself, I can claim to be the innovator and designer with the imagination and will to bring new projects into being. As chairman, mine is the ultimate responsibility for our financial needs and problems, although in practice most of the decisions are agreed between the three of us.

It must be very unusual for three people to agree so often. It happens because we have very similar ideas about what Cranks should be like. As we approach our sixties, we wonder about our future and that of those combined beliefs that became the institution of Cranks.

So many people ask us why we chose the name 'Cranks'. It was not because we considered ourselves, as the dictionary puts it, 'faddists', but because we wanted a label to show that with strong vegetarian and wholefood principles, we were very different from the orthodox retail and catering establishment and we wanted a light-hearted, humorous approach.

Nowadays healthy eating is no longer seen as 'cranky' – perhaps we are seen as unusual for our tenacity in sticking to the best ingredients, labour-intensive methods and craftsman-made surroundings despite their soaring costs.

These are things worth fighting for, and fortunately our many supporters show they enjoy them as much as we do. Cranks couldn't exist without the support of those who work for us – now some 200 people – and those who eat with us. That sense of community is another element of the lovely spirit of Cranks. Tasting is believing!

List of recipes

Soups

Bran water & oatmeal water
  to use as stock
Creamy onion soup
Green pea soup
Cream of watercress soup
Mangetout soup
Borscht
Cream of leek soup
Cream of spinach & courgette
  soup
Fresh tomato soup
Apple & peanut butter soup
Mushroom soup
Mulligatawny soup
Creamy potato soup
Carrot potage
Buckwheat & potato soup
Carrot, apple & cashew nut
  soup
Armenian soup
Egg & lemon soup
Cheddar cheese soup
Celery & cashew nut soup
Parsnip & apple soup
Cauliflower soup
Potage Malakoff
Russian vegetable soup
Pumpkin & spinach soup

French onion soup
Country vegetable soup
Lentil & tomato soup
Chunky bean soup
Hauser soup
Gazpacho

Salads

Carrot mayonnaise
Coleslaw
Cucumber in tarragon
  dressing
Waldorf salad
Spinach & mushroom salad
Beetroot, celery & orange
  salad
Potato salad
Carrot & swede in soured
  cream dressing
Celery & apple salad
Wholewheat mayonnaise
Hawaiian rice salad
Creamy beetroot salad
Leek salad
Italian pasta salad
Bulghur salad
Celery, cucumber & grape
  salad

Tomato & cheese pizza
Macaroni cheese with
    vegetables
Mushroom burgers
Moussaka
Spicy chick peas
Eggs Florentine
Aubergine Parmesan
Millet & vegetable gratinée
Lentil & buckwheat slice
Golden vegetable layer
Oriental beanshoots
Mushroom Stroganoff
Vegetarian goulash
Express cheese pudding
Curried split peas
Haricot beans in tomato
    sauce
Winter hot pot
'Macro' rice
Savoury mix
Lentil & cheese wedges
Surrey raised pie
Soya mix – using T.S.P.
Soya, egg & vegetable pie
Soya 'burgers' in salad baps
Buckwheat pancakes
Stir-fried leeks with
    mushrooms
Cauliflower cheese
Buckwheat bake
Savoury potato dish
Spiced chick pea croquettes
'No-cook rissoles'
Stuffed cabbage leaves
Creamy leek croustade
Spinach roulade
Stuffed peppers
Cheese, onion & tomato flan

Stuffed aubergines
Homity pies
Crecy plate pie
Crispy mushroom layer
Aubergine & red bean stew
Country pasties
Vegetable crumble
Cheese & millet croquettes
Leak & cheese flan

Biscuits

Cranks flapjack
Melting moments
Eccles cakes
Date slices
Carob crunch
Shortbread
Country biscuits
Coconut biscuits
Carob chip cookies
Florentines
Sesame thins
Millet & peanut cookies
Caraway bran biscuits
Crunchies
Peanut rounds
Gingernuts
Cheesejacks
Cheese biscuits
Wholemeal rusks
Melba toast

Breakfast cereals

Breakfast cereal
Muesli
Milled wholewheat berries &
    nuts

Bread

Cranks wholemeal bread
Corn & molasses bread
Rye bread
Bran bread
Barley bread
Soya bread
Sourdough bread
Cheese bread
Garlic bread
Cheese baps
Herb bread
Granary cob
Four grain bread
Pumpernickel
Unyeasted bread
Oatmeal soda bread
Apple & banana bread
Spiced currant bread
Walnut tea bread
Hot cross buns
Jam doughnuts
Chelsea buns

Puddings & desserts

Creamy yoghourt flan
Banana yoghourt flan
Puréed fruit jelly
Lemon cheesecake
Lemon meringue pie
Sticky prune cake
Raw sugar jam tart
Baked egg custard
Orange & banana trifle
Creamy bran & apple chunks
Apple pie
Bakewell tart

Spiced bread pudding
Tangy apple swirl
Grape & banana flan
Junket
'Toffeed' rhubarb fool
Custard tart
Walnut pie
Hazelnut & black cherry tart
Carrageen citrus jelly
Devon apple cake
Carob blancmange
Brandied prune mousse
Buttermilk dessert
Honey & apple tart
Date & apple squares
Treacle tart
Apple crumble
Bread & butter pudding
Baked apples
Pouding Alsace
Mincemeat & apple 'jalousie'
Home-made yoghourt
Christmas pudding

Cakes & scones

Belgian cake
Old-fashioned ginger cake
100% wholemeal sponge
Swiss roll
Christmas cake
Almond paste
Mock marzipan
Brown sugar icing
Luscious lemon cake
Carob cake
Date & coconut gateau
Carrot cake
Honey cake

Poppyseed cake
Walnut sandwich cake
Simnel cake
Orange cake
Date & walnut loaf
Orange ginger cake
Fruit cake without eggs
Barabrith
Wholemeal muffins
Bran muffins
Apple buns
Old English rock buns
Raspberry buns
Walnut bars
Chocolate éclairs
Fruit scones
Drop scones
Cheese scones
Brown sugar meringues
Welsh butter cakes
Coconut castles
Honey buns
Truffle triangle

Pastry

Wholemeal shortcrust pastry

Hot water crust pastry
Choux pastry
Wholemeal pastry made with
  oil

Preserves & sweetmeats

Coarse-cut orange
  marmalade
Lemon curd
Apple butter
Apple & ginger chutney
Fruit and nut chews
Marzipan shapes
Coconut bars
Carob 'fudge'
Dried apricot & almond
  jam

Drinks

Freshly extracted vegetable &
  fruit juices
Preparation for extracted
  juices
Recipes for drinks as served
  at Cranks

Culinary know-how

What you need to know about the health foods and their preparation before you start to cook.

Flours & pasta

100% Wholemeal flour. This is flour in nature's complete form, with all the valuable vitamins, minerals and trace elements contained in the outer husk (bran) and central wheatgerm, as well as the protein and starch content. The best wholemeal flour is that which has been milled by stone (stoneground) rather than by steel rollers used by the large millers, and which has been grown 'organically', without the use of chemical fertilizers. This flour is available either in this plain form, or as 'self-raising' when it has added raising agents.

In Cranks bakeries we use only 100% wholemeal flour in all our products, except of course for barley and rye bread. Although our Cranks Health Loaf is made in such a way as to achieve the close, moist texture of the Grant Loaf, the method has to be geared to the large production.

85% Wholemeal flour. To arrive at an 85% flour the whole grain is milled in such a way as to remove most of the bran, amounting to 15% of the bulk. This produces a finer and paler flour of less nutritional value than 100%, but nevertheless of very much greater value than white flour which has had most of its food value removed and has also been adulterated with chemical additives to achieve a high degree of whiteness. The 85% flour is also available plain or in 'self-raising' form.

Soya flour. Made from the ground soya bean, this is a fine, pale flour. It is a rich protein source, and can be added to wheat bread dough to give additional food value and to help keep it moist. It can also be used to make mock marzipan (*see page 178*) and Bakewell tart (*see page 157*).

Rye flour. Made from milled rye grains, it may be dark or light depending on the removal of bran. It is most suitable for bread doughs, although rye bread will be flatter than wheat because of the lower gluten content. Rye flour is rich in vitamins and minerals, with a 12% protein content, and is low in gluten.

Barley flour. Made from milled barley grains, it is very pale in colour and fine textured. It is normally used in conjunction with wheat flour and is suitable for bread and biscuits and to thicken sauces.

Maize flour (CORN MEAL). Corn kernels are ground to a coarse or fine pale yellow meal. Use as a thickening agent or in breads and puddings.

Rice flour. Unpolished or brown rice is milled and ground to produce fine, medium or coarse flours. Use in biscuits or as a thickening agent.

Gluten-free flour. Gluten-free flours are available for those on a special diet.

Buckwheat flour. Ground buckwheat produces a fine, dark, speckled flour. Used particularly in batters.

Wholemeal pasta. Available in a wide range of shapes, this is made from 100% wholemeal flour or buckwheat flour.

Cereals & grains

Barley. The chief bread grain of the Hebrews, Greeks and Romans, and of much of Europe until modern times. Pearl barley has had the outer layers and germ removed, while pot barley has had only the indigestible husk removed.

Wheat. This has been the principal cereal grain of Europe and the New East for thousands of years. Modern wheats are of three main types:

Bread wheats are high in gluten-forming proteins.

Soft wheats are low in gluten and give a light texture to cakes, biscuits and pastry.

Durum wheats are the hardest and are used to make pasta products. Wholewheat berries add a mild, nutty flavour to soups and stews, and make an ideal base for salads and breakfast cereals. Flaked wheat is also available.

Oats. Higher in protein and oil than other grains, oats were originally wild plants considered to be weeds. They were then domesticated and used in the harsh climate of northern Europe and are well suited to our cold, damp English winters. Oats are more commonly used as oatmeal, which is the whole grain rolled or cut into flakes, available in fine, medium and coarse meal.

Rye. This hardy grain is often cultivated where high altitudes, cold temperatures or poor soil discourages other grains. In Eastern Europe rye flour is particularly popular, but less so in Britain.

Buckwheat. Not a grain, but the seeds of the plant sometimes known as Saracen corn. Rich in protein and minerals, it contains most of the vitamin B complex. Also available ready-roasted.

Millet. Dating back to prehistoric times, millet is richer in vitamins, mineral and fat content than any other grain. The grain has its protective, uneatable husk removed before use. It has a high protein content and is easily digested. Also available as flakes.

Bulghur. A preparation of wheat used in Middle Eastern cooking. It is made by cooking wheat, then drying and cracking it. Bulghur comes in varying degrees of coarseness and has excellent nutritional value as a good source of phosphorus, iron and B vitamins.

Rice. This has been a staple food for thousands of years in Asia, China, Spain and Italy and is grown extensively in the East, as well as France, Eastern Europe, Australia and the USA. It is the largest food crop in the world. Rice is similar in structure to wheat, and goes through a process of milling which removes the outer husk, leaving a brownish grain which is the bran-covered rice. This bran is removed to give white rice (known as polished rice). Whole (brown) rice retains all the valuable minerals and vitamins and is a good source of starch. Its protein content is lower than that of other grains. Brown rices takes a little longer to cook than white rice and has a delicious nutty flavour. Adding some oil or a knob of butter to the water in which the rice is boiled avoids the tendency of the rice to cook into a coagulated mass.

Wheatgerm. As the name implies, this is the actual germ of the wheat, the part from which the new plant springs. The most nutritious wheatgerm is unstabilized, but it follows that it has a more limited shelf life than the stabilized product. It is an extremely valuable source of vitamin E, as well as part of the vitamin B complex and minerals, including iron. Its main value is the yield of vitamin E which can be obtained in the form of oil.

Bran. The protective, tough outer cover of the wheat grain. It is milled together with the rest of the grain to make 100% wholemeal flour, but can also be separated from the grain and used as supplementary roughage in the diet. It is a rich source of protein, vitamin B complex and phosphorus and valued for its high fibre content.

Arrowroot. This is the white starch extracted from the rhizome of a herbaceous perennial plant, indigenous in West

Indian islands and possibly Central America. It is now grown in Bengal, Java, the Philippines, Mauritius, Natal and West Africa. It is used as a thickening agent, and considered to be useful in remedying digestive disorders.

Pulses & beans

Lentils. These are grown in the Mediterranean region and were used in early days by the Greeks and Egyptians. The seeds are dried, dehusked and sometimes split and are either orange-red or greenish-brown in colour. They have a high protein content and are quite easily digested.

Chick peas. A pulse crop of India, now grown in America, Africa and Australia. Creamy yellow in colour and mealy in texture when cooked. A good source of protein.

Dried beans. These are rich in iron, potassium and vitamin B complex and low in carbohydrate and fat. They also contain a high fibre content and so provide essential roughage within the diet.

There are many different types of bean available. These include:

Flageolets. Pale green in colour with an elongated bean shape.

Red kidney beans. Dark red in colour, larger than the haricot.

WARNING: It has recently been discovered that there is a poisonous substance in red kidney beans which is only destroyed when they are fast boiled for at least 10 minutes.

Haricot beans. White in colour, a fairly small bean.

Split peas. Split dried peas with the skin removed.

All these beans must be soaked before cooking.
Cooking times will vary according to type and age.
Do not add salt during boiling as this will toughen the skins.

Seeds

Sesame. Grown mainly in Africa, Asia and South America, these seeds are white or brown in colour. The seeds contain almost 50% oil, are high in protein and a good source of vitamin B complexs and minerals, particularly calcium.

Sunflower. Grown mainly in Russia and the USA, they are particularly rich in vitamin B complex and a good source of minerals and protein.

Caraway. A plant, native to the Mediterranean shores, but now indigenous all over Europe. Grown largely for its aromatic seeds.

Alfalfa. A plant which is rich in protein and minerals, including iron, calcium and magnesium, and is a source of vitamins B12 and K.

Some seeds, such as bean sprouts, alfalfa and lentils, can be easily sprouted at home in jars and are ready to eat in 3–6 days. They are a valuable source of fresh vitamins all the year round. Sprouting seeds can be bought from health food shops.

Dried fruits

Dried fruits are rich in natural sugar (fructose) and are often much sweeter than their fresh counterpart because the fruits are left on the trees to ripen for a greater length of time. They are also rich in minerals such as potassium and iron and vitamins A and B. Processing techniques vary, but usually the fruit is picked, halved, pitted or left whole according to type, and then dried. Sun drying is the most suitable method of drying, but artificial heat is sometimes used. Other methods include the use of sulphur dioxide or freeze-drying.

Apricots. These contain a considerable amount of vitamin C and A. First grown in Northern Asia, they are now imported from South Africa, Australia and Turkey. Colour and flavour vary with country of origin.

Dates. Available with or without the stone, dates are imported from North Africa and California. Eaten both fresh and dry, they are a wonderful instance of nature's sweetening, containing vitamins A, B1 and B2. An easily digested energy food.

Prunes. They are high in vitamins A and B. The best plums for drying are 'Santa Clara', which are American but are also imported from South America and Australia.

Currants. These are the dried fruit of a tiny purple grape which are sharper in flavour than sultanas or raisins. They are mainly imported from Greece.

Raisins. Known since Biblical times, they are rich in iron and copper, and available in two sorts: stoned or seeded (when the pips have been removed) and seedless (from grapes which have no pips). Stoned raisins are larger and considered superior. Raisins are imported from Spain, Australia, America and South Africa.

Sultanas. They come from a seedless grape, are much sweeter than either currants or raisins, and should be light in colour and fleshy. They are imported from Australia, South Africa, Turkey and parts of the Mediterranean.

All dried fruits should be thoroughly washed before using.

Nuts

Almond. The kernel of the fruit of the almond tree, widely grown in California.

Brazil nut. The fruit of a large tree, grown originally in Brazil – hence the name. The segment-like nuts fit together in a similar way to an orange, and are encased in an outer husk rather like a coconut shell.

Cashew nut. The kidney-shaped seeds of a tropical tree native to Brazil, but now grown in India and East Africa. The fruit is like a large fleshy apple and has a nut hanging below it containing the kernel, which is manually extracted after roasting.

Chestnut. Large brown nut of a native Mediterranean tree.

Coconut. The fruit of the coconut palm, consisting of the inner husk containing the white coconut and milk. It originated in Malaya but is now grown in most tropical regions of the world. The white flesh is dried and grated to make desiccated coconut.

Walnut. The fruit of the walnut tree. The walnut has a smooth, outer green husk which is removed when the ripe nuts are picked. The outer shell is removed and only the kernel is eaten.

Peanut. Sometimes known as the groundnut, it is not a true nut but comes in the pod of a leguminous plant, which grows underground. There are two kernels in each pod. Peanuts are grown extensively in Africa and South America.

Sugar, sweeteners & preserves

Raw brown sugar. Raw brown sugar is a natural product from unrefined cane sugar. It does not contain any artificial colourings or additives of any sort. Raw sugar is always produced in the country of origin, and if this is not stated on the packet it is not the 'real' thing. It comes in four types:

Demerara. This has clear, sparkling crystals of a large, consistent size. It also has a crunchy yet sticky texture and rich aroma because of its natural molasses. It takes its name from Demerara, Guyana, where it was first produced.

Muscovado. Sometimes called Barbados sugar, this is a soft, sticky, fine-grained, dark brown sugar, rich in natural molasses.

Light Muscovado. A creamy-coloured soft cane sugar.

Molasses Sugar. Also known as Black Barbados or Demerara Molasses. Stronger in flavour than Muscovado because of the greater molasses content, it is sticky and almost black and is very rich in minerals and trace elements.

Store raw brown sugars in a lidded jar. If the sugar becomes solid, add a small piece of cut raw potato to the storage jar or place the packet of sugar in a polythene bag with the piece of cut raw potato and seal it. Before using it in cooking always 'pick over' the sugar to remove any large lumps. Alternatively, push it through a sieve or blend in a liquidizer goblet.

Molasses. A thick, dark syrup left over when sugar cane is refined. Molasses is a good source of vitamin B, and particularly rich in iron.

Honey. A natural product made from the nectar of flowers. Bees collect the nectar and its structure of sugars is processed by the enzymes present in the bee's stomach. It is then stored in the honeycomb where the sugar conversion continues to produce the product known as honey, which is a fragile, delicately balanced mixture of carbohydrates in water, with fat, protein, enzymes, vitamins, amino acids and aromatic compounds. The flavour of each honey will vary with the differing balance of these constituents, the flowers from which the nectar was collected, the weather and natural variation.

Honey is very easily digested and so is a good, quick source of energy. It can be used in place of sugar as a sweetening agent, but care must be taken when using it in cake mixtures, as it has a strong and distinctive flavour, so follow a recipe.

Preserves. Jams, sweet mincemeat and marmalade can be made with raw brown sugar, and are available from health food stores. See recipes in the Preserves chapter.

Oils

These are an essential part of the diet. They contain acids (essential fatty acids) which cannot be manufactured by the body and must be provided in the diet. They play a significant part in cell structure and can assist in the remedy of skin ailments. They contain vitamins A, D, E and K. Most health stores concentrate on the sale of sunflower, safflower, soya and corn oils. These all contain a high percentage of poly-unsaturated fatty acids which make them desirable for use in diets where coronary disease is a consideration or preventative measures are necessary. Groundnut and olive oils are not suitable for this purpose. Sesame oil is also available.

Unrefined oils are the first choice of health-conscious people because they consist of the first 30% of oil extracted from the seeds, beans or grains by 'cold pressing'. The residual mash left from the pressing then has some 70% of its weight extracted as oil by being dissolved in a chemical solvent which is later removed.

Nutter

A carefully balanced mixture of nut oils which produces a vegetarian shortening alternative to lard.

Butter

This is produced from milk, and usually contains more then 80% butterfat. It also contains vitamins A and D, and small amounts of protein, milk sugar and minerals.

Tomor

The trade name for margarine, made from pure vegetable oils, and suitable for vegans. Many margarines may contain a mixture of marine, animal and vegetable oils and possibly whey, so are not suitable for a strict vegetarian diet.

Cheese

Cottage cheese. This is a type of curd cheese, made from skimmed milk with the addition of rennet. The resulting curds are cut and washed to produce the familiar 'granular' and creamy texture. Cream is often added for a richer product.

Curd cheese. This soft, smooth cheese can be made by simply allowing the milk to 'turn' naturally, but it is more usually made by adding a lactic starter to the milk. The resulting curds and whey are separated, and the curds become known as curd cheese.

Cream cheese. This is made by a similar process to that for curd cheese, but cream and not milk is used as the basic ingredient. The cream is cultured with either a lactic starter or a rennet, and the resulting curds and whey are strained to give cream cheese. It is obviously richer than curd and cottage cheeses.

Skimmed milk cheese. Skimmed milk is milk which has had the cream removed from it and is therefore virtually free from fat. Curd cheese made from this is highly favoured in a healthy and slimming diet.

Hard cheeses, e.g. Cheddar, Double Gloucester. Hard cheeses made with a vegetarian rennet, as opposed to an animal rennet, are available in most health food shops.

Cream, milk & yoghourt

Soured cream. This is actually cultured and not soured. Single cream is treated in a similar way to milk when making yoghourt by adding a 'live' cheese culture to it.

Fresh dairy cream. This may be untreated, in which case it should be bought and used as quickly as possible.

Pasteurized cream has undergone heat-treatment, a process which destroys bacteria and prolongs its keeping qualities but also reduces its nutritional value. It is available as single, double, whipping or, in the west country, as clotted. The thickness of cream varies with the butterfat content.

Skimmed milk. This is milk with enough of the cream content 'skimmed' off to leave a fat content of not more than 0.3%.

Skimmed milk powder. Milk powder is produced by the evaporation of water from milk by heat, or other means, to produce solids containing 5% or less moisture. Skimmed milk powder contains virtually no fat, and therefore no fat-soluble vitamins, but it does contain protein, calcium and riboflavin.

Yoghourt. This is produced from milk by the introduction of two organisms – *Lactobacillus bulgaricus* and *Streptococcus thermophilus* – which cause fermentation of the lactic acid within the milk. When a carton of yoghourt indicates that the contents are 'live', this means that the bacillus bulgaricus remains active within the yoghourt with a resulting beneficial effect on the digestive processes assisted by the production of vitamin B within the body. It is an excellent source of protein, and provides a significant quantity of calcium, so always buy 'live' yoghourt ready to eat or to use as a 'starter' for home-made yoghourt (*see page 170*).

Buttermilk. There are two sorts of buttermilk:

(a) The liquid left over when butter is produced from milk.

(b) A cultured milk which is made from separated milk. The method is similar to that of yoghourt-making. A culture is introduced to the milk, which is then heated. The resulting buttermilk is much thicker than type (a).

Soya milk. This is 'milk' produced from soya flour and is therefore valuable for vegans as an alternative to cows' milk.

Granolac is a hypo-allergic soya infant formula. It is fibre-free and well-balanced in protein, soya fat and carbohydrates. It is easily digested and can be used as an alternative to cows' milk.

Cider vinegar

This is considered by naturopaths and other experts to be more beneficial to health than either malt or wine vinegar. To some extent this view seems to emerge from the folk medicine tradition. Undoubtedly cider vinegar is rich in the mineral salts, particularly potassium, and these have a very beneficial effect on the body's metabolism. It is thought that the combination of the acetic acid produced by the conversion of the cider into vinegar, and the citric acid from the apples, quickly metabolizes in the body and so produces a significant alkaline increase and therefore an improvement in the vital alkaline/acid balance in the bloodstream. This is helpful in many disorders of the body, particularly arthritis. The cider vinegar used in Cranks comes from Aspall Hall in Suffolk and is made from organically grown apples.

Soya sauce

The use and manufacture of soya sauce has been known in China since the sixth century. There may be some confusion between the various types of soya sauce on the market. Tamari is a term which has been used to describe soya sauce which is naturally fermented and made without the use of chemicals. Soya sauce is made from a mixture of wheat and soya beans, which has been soaked until soft, slightly cooked with water and sea salt and then inoculated with 'koji' bacteria to promote fermentation. After the mash is pressed and the liquid extracted, the soya sauce is quickly heated to slow down the fermentation and preserve the flavour.

TSP (Textured soya protein)

This is a processed soya bean product used in vegetarian cooking as an alternative source of protein. It is available in dehydrated form as 'mince' or in chunks. This is sold under various trade names and stocked in most health food stores.

Natural essences

A whole range of natural essences is available from health food stores. These essences are completely free from synthetic substances. Flavours include almond, vanilla, ginger and peppermint.

Jelling compounds

(The vegetarian alternative to gelatine, which is derived from animal carcases.)

Carrageen. A particular type of seaweed which can be bought in packets in a dried form and used for thickening stews, soups, jellies and so on. Follow the instructions on the packet.

Gelozone. A starch-free jelling agent made from a special preparation of Irish moss and Carrageen moss. Used to thicken hot drinks, soups and sauces.

Agar-agar. A jelling compound derived from seaweed which produces a cloudy jelly, not a clear one as with the usual packet variety of tablet jelly or gelatine.

Carob

Carob beans are the fruit of the carob tree, usually found in warm climates such as Spain, Greece, Cyprus, Italy and Morocco. They look like dark brown, shiny runner beans, but are very hard. The ripe beans (pods) are crushed and the pulpy portion of the beans is separated from the hard seeds. This is ground to a powder, which may be substituted in any recipe which calls for cocoa or chocolate powder. It is also available in a bar, as an alternative to chocolate. Although processed carob and chocolate look alike and taste alike, carob is more than a mere substitute. It is rich in vitamins and minerals and, unlike chocolate, contains no refined sugar or habit-forming caffeine.

Rennet

Vegetarian rennet is available for making cheese and junket. It is made from a microbial enzyme, and in some cases from an extract of French mushrooms. (Animal rennet is derived from the stomach of a calf.)

Vegetable stock cubes

Available with or without salt, these are made from vegetable fat, yeast extract, lactose, hydrolized vegetable protein, sunflower oil, vegetables and spices.

Yeast

A great variety of yeasts exist in nature as living cells, and some are specially suited for yeast cookery. These selected and specially bred strains of yeast are isolated and cultivated scientifically and sold as compressed yeast. This active yeast is also dried in such a way that the cells will remain active after many months of storage in a cool place. This is Dried Baking Yeast and is usually sold in small packets or tins. Dried yeast can be used instead of fresh yeast and is equally successful for breadmaking. Use half the weight of dried yeast to fresh, i.e. if a recipe indicates 1 oz (25 g) fresh yeast, use ½ oz (15 g) dried yeast. Always follow the instructions on the tin or packet on how to reconstitute or incorporate the dried yeast into the flour.

There are also other kinds of dried yeast which are inactive and will not raise bread. These have a valuable source of vitamin B which, in a powdered or flaked form, may be sprinkled over cereals, added to baked goods, such as bread, or consumed in tablet form as a diet supplement.

Brewer's yeast. This is a by-product of the brewing process and is sold in powdered and tablet form. It has been found to contain seventeen vitamins, including all the B vitamins and fourteen minerals, including the essential 'trace' elements. It also contains 36% protein.

Yeast extract. When brewer's yeast is mixed with salt it is broken down by its own enzymes. The soluble residue is evaporated to produce yeast extract, familiar as a sticky brown substance. There are a number of different brands available, varying in flavour with individual ingredients. The best one is made from a vegetable concentrate, containing seaweed, which is rich in minerals.

Preparation of fruit & vegetables for cooking

In most fruit and vegetables the vitamins and minerals are stored in or just below the skin. For this reason, at Cranks we do not peel fruit or vegetables, but simply wash or scrub them. However, there are obvious exceptions such as onions and garlic which need to be skinned, and fruit like bananas and pineapple which must be peeled.

In some cases, as when making purées, it is preferable to remove outer skins. There is no need to throw these peelings away – both vegetable and fruit peelings should be reserved. They can then be simmered separately in water, strained, covered and stored in a refrigerator to use as required. Vegetable water can be used as stock or as a base for drinks, while fruit-flavoured water can be used to make a fruit syrup for salad, used as a drink, or can be set with jelling compound. Citrus fruit peel, or halves, should be kept and dried out in the oven. To do this, place the fruit halves cut-side down on a baking sheet. Place in a cool oven and leave for several hours until completely moisture free. Crumble the peel into small pieces and grind in a coffee mill. Sieve and store the resulting powder in an airtight container, and use to add to cakes, biscuits, puddings, and so on to give added flavour.

The quantity of fruit and vegetables in all recipes indicates their weight prior to preparation. They must then be scrubbed, washed or trimmed, as necessary, ready for use, as follows:

apples, pears, etc.	wash and core
plums, grapes, apricots, etc.	wash, remove stones or pips
banana, pineapple, etc.	peel or cut away the skin
citrus fruits	peel and cut away white pith if wished

root vegetables	scrub and trim
leafy vegetables and herbs	wash and discard any discoloured leaves
peppers	cut in half, discard stem and remove seeds
mushrooms	wash or wipe, do not peel
celery	separate sticks, scrub and trim
leeks	trim, clean thoroughly to remove soil

Herbs

Whenever possible use fresh herbs in cooking. Simply wash and dry the herb to be used and chop it. When using dried herbs, do remember that the flavour is more concentrated and a lesser amount should be added. Dried herbs may be reconstituted in a little warm water before use.

The use of salt & pepper in the cooking & preparation of food

Salt. Ordinary table or 'common' salt is almost pure sodium chloride, which could cause an imbalance if taken in the quantities given in the recipes. At Cranks we use only 'Biosalt', and recommend that you use this or sea salt. We also suggest that you follow the quantities of salt in the recipes carefully and make a note of any adjustment you might want to make to suit your taste.

Pepper. Black pepper is a whole berry. The outer husk of the ripe berry is removed to produce white peppercorns. These are both ground to give the resulting black and white peppers.

Freezing of food

Specific instructions for freezing are not included in this book, but this does not mean that particular recipes are unsuitable for freezing. There are many good books available on this subject which will supply all the necessary details on suitability of foods for freezing and how to package them. As a general rule, breads and baked goods freeze particularly well – soups and savouries too, providing they do not contain cream. Flavourings, especially garlic, are affected by freezing, which considerably reduces their storage time to a maximum of three weeks.

Metrication

The recipes in this book have been metricated and written up using a 25 g unit to correspond approximately to 1 oz (28.3g). For this reason it is essential to follow either the metric column or the imperial column and *not to alternate between the two* as this may jeopardize the result.

Food manufacturers now metricate their packaging, so always check the weight of a pack before using it. A pint of milk, however, is 568 ml (rather than 600 ml) and, to simplify using this or cartons of cream or yoghourt, for all fluid dairy products we have kept the measurements exact.

British Standard Institute measure spoons of 15 ml (1 tbsp), 5 ml (1 tsp), 2.5 ml (½ tsp) and 1.25 ml (¼ tsp) have been used in all these recipes.

US equivalent measures

US cups	British terms (approx.)	US cups	British terms (approx.)
1 tsp	1 tsp	2 cups (1 pt)	¾ pt
1 tbsp	1 tbsp	2½ cups	1 pt
¼ cup	4 tbsp	3 cups	1⅕ pts
⅓ cup	5 tbsp	4 cups (1 qt)	1½ pts
½ cup	⅕ pt		
⅔ cup	¼ pt	6 cups (1½ qts)	2½ pts
¾ cup	6 oz		
1 cup	8 oz	8 cups (2 qts)	3¼ pts
1¼ cups	½ pt		
1⅓ cups	½ pt	2½ qts	4 pts
1½ cups	12 oz	3 qts	5 pts
1⅔ cups	13 oz	4 qts	6½ pts
1¾ cups	¾ pt		

The use of a minute timer

All the recipes in this book have been tested and their cooking times checked. Although there may be slight variations in temperature with different types of ovens, it is always advisable to use a timer when following a recipe.

Oven temperature guide

	Electric °F	Gas mark	Electric °C
Very cool	225–250	¼–½	110–130
Cool	275–300	1–2	140–150
Warm	325	3	170
Moderate	350	4	180
Fairly hot	375–400	5–6	190–200
Hot	425	7	220
Very hot	450–475	8–9	230–240

Cooking terms

To bake 'blind'. Baking pastry cases without a filling. To do this, cut a circle of greaseproof paper about 5 cm (2″) larger than the pastry case and place this inside the pastry case. Fill with dried beans and bake as per recipe. Keep the beans for future use.

To pare. Referring to citrus fruit rind. To remove the outer zest of the fruit in a thin strip. This is most easily done with a potato peeler or small sharp knife.

To toast. Referring to desiccated coconut or cereals. Lay the coconut or cereal on a shallow baking sheet and brown, turning frequently, under a medium hot grill or in a fairly hot oven, until evenly golden.

To whisk. Adding one ingredient to another to produce an evenly combined mixture, or incorporating air into a mixture, i.e. into egg whites for meringues, using either a fork, balloon whisk or electric mixer.

To dice. To cut into small cubes.

To shred. To slice finely using a sharp knife or coarse grater.

To hard boil. Referring to eggs. Place eggs in a saucepan of boiling water and simmer gently for 10 minutes. Plunge immediately into cold water and allow to cool before removing shell.

To steam. Usually of fruit, vegetables and sometimes bread. A method of cooking utilizing the steam from boiling water. This can be done in a steamer, or in a pudding basin inside a saucepan of water.

To sauté. Usually referring to vegetables. To fry quickly in hot fat, stirring frequently to prevent sticking.

To crush. Referring to garlic. Peel garlic clove and either push through a garlic press or place on a chopping board, sprinkle with a little salt and, using the flat side of a knife blade, squash the garlic to a paste.

Referring to biscuits. Place biscuits in a polythene bag and reduce to crumbs with a rolling pin.

To blend. To purée in a liquidizer goblet until smooth. Care should be taken that the food is cool before blending, otherwise a build-up of steam will produce a vacuum and the lid will blow off!

To make wholemeal breadcrumbs. Cut stale wholemeal bread into small pieces and rub through a sieve, or reduce to crumbs in a liquidizer goblet.

To toast crumbs, spread the fresh breadcrumbs on a shallow baking sheet and toast under a medium hot grill, turning occasionally, or dry out in a moderate oven until crisp.

To blanch. To plunge food into boiling water, usually to preserve its natural colour, to remove a flavour which is too strong or to soften the texture of the food.

To marinate. To soak food in a blend of liquids such as oil, vinegar or lemon juice and seasonings to give flavour to that food.

To 'top and tail'. Referring to vegetables such as beans or radishes. To trim them at each end to remove stalks, leaves, etc.

To rise. Referring to yeasted doughs. To leave dough in a warm place, covered with oiled polythene until the dough has doubled in size, or until it has reached the top of the tin.

To knead. Usually of bread dough or pastry. To work the dough by hand, or using the dough hook of an electric mixer, in a continuous circular movement, to produce a smooth dough. In the case of bread dough, kneading is essential to ensure an even texture throughout the finished bread.

To fold in. To incorporate two mixtures carefully together using a large metal spoon, or spatula, in a figure-of-eight movement. This is usually required when adding an ingredient or mixture to another mixture which is highly aerated to prevent excessive loss of air, and consequent lightness in the finished dish, e.g. adding flour to a whisked egg and sugar mixture when making a whisked egg sponge.

Containers to cook in

There is evidence to suggest that there is a poisonous release from aluminium cooking vessels which causes harmful reactions in the body. Cranks strongly recommends the use of stainless steel or good quality enamel or iron in place of aluminium. See the Bibliography (*page 43*) for a book with more information on this subject.

Pressure cookers. Pressure cooking is a quick and efficient method of cooking, but just because it is so fast it is very necessary to time carefully to avoid overcooking. It is possible to get stainless steel pressure cookers.

Steamers. It is suprising that cooking in a steamer is a method not more commonly used. In Cranks we are very much in favour of this method because it ensures that the maximum goodness and flavour is retained within the food.

Petal steamers, which are adjustable to fit various sizes of saucepan, are widely available and can be very useful, particularly for fruit and vegetables. Conventional steamers can be used very effectively for the cooking of puddings and specialized breads.

Bibliography

From the huge variety of books now written on health, diet and nutrition, we have singled out a few special ones, some of which we feel have now become classics in their own right. A number of the books may not always be available and in such instances we suggest you refer to your local library.

SILENT SPRING by Rachel Carson
A passionate scientific exposure of the effects of the indiscriminate use of insecticides on wildlife and on the balance of nature – and of man's progressive poisoning of his own habitat.

LOOK YOUNGER, LIVE LONGER by Gaylord Hauser
A book full of valuable advice from this famous nutritionist, revealing his secrets for good food, good health and good looks.

YOUR DAILY FOOD (A Recipe for Survival) by Doris Grant
Well-documented and convincing, this book explains fully the hazards and dangers of modern living and the decline in our food which has become increasingly contaminated, and offers practical advice on how to avoid them.

ANIMAL MACHINES by Ruth Harrison
A penetrating indictment on intensive factory farming methods.

SMALL IS BEAUTIFUL by Dr E. F. Schumacher
'Economics as if people mattered.' The book which has earned Dr Schumacher such world-wide recognition. It provides an

important basis to Schumacher's thinking and is a guide to the main issues which concerned him, such as appropriate technology, energy policies, industrial ownership and organization.

THE HOMOEOPATHIC HANDBOOK edited by T. M. Cook (Nelson)
A most useful book listing homoeopathic doctors, homoeopathic organizations, and general homoeopathic medicine for home treatment of common illnesses/diseases.

THE BIOCHEMIC HANDBOOK
An introduction to the cellular therapy and practical application of the 12 tissue cell-salts in accordance with the biochemic system of medicine originated by Dr W. H. Schuessler.

FOOD FOR FREE by Richard Mabey
A guide to the edible wild plants of Britain.

NATURE CURE IN A NUTSHELL by Tom W. Moule
A small, concise handbook of practical hints for healthful living based on nature cure and diet reform principles.

ARTHRITIS AND FOLK MEDICINE by D. C. Jarvis
Commonsense practical suggestions for helping to relieve arthritis and allied complaints, based on nature's laws.

COOKING FOR SPECIAL DIETS by Bee Nilson
A comprehensive guide for providing meals for those on special diets.

HAVING A BABY EASILY by Margaret Brady
Practical advice on all aspects of child care, with dietary advice for pregnancy and the post-natal period.

THE COMPLETE HOME GUIDE TO ALL THE VITAMINS by Ruth Adams
All you want to know about vitamins.

WHY ALUMINIUM PANS ARE DANGEROUS by Edgar J. Saxon
Facts regarding the hazards of aluminium pans.

63 MEATLESS MEALS by Bridget Amies
A practical selection of recipes to help you prepare balanced meals.

CHILDREN'S DIET by Bircher-Benner
Bircher-Benner's principles of diet as applied to children.

EVERYBODY'S GUIDE TO NATURE CURE by Harry Benjamin
A complete guide to the principles of naturopathy.

BETTER SIGHT WITHOUT GLASSES by Harry Benjamin
How to improve your sight with diet and exercise.

WHAT'S COOKING by Eva Batt
The vegan guide to good eating.

THE OXFORD BOOK OF FOOD PLANTS by G. B. Masefield, M. Wallis, S. G. Harrison & B. E. Nicholson
A colourfully illustrated book describing 420 different plants which serve the human race for food.

HERBS FOR HEALTH AND COOKERY by Claire Loewenfeld & Philippa Back
All about herbs and how to use them.

THE USES OF JUICES by C. E. Clinkard
Information regarding the inestimable value of freshly extracted raw fruit and vegetable juices and the purpose for which each juice is used.

A–Z OF HEALTH FOODS by Carol Bowen
A handy A–Z glossary providing information on the use, preparation, cooking instructions and storage of health foods, together with a recipe section.

HEALTHY EATING FOR THE NEW AGE by Joyce d'Silva
Excellent and varied recipes which adhere to health foods as
well as vegan principles.

PRESCRIPTION FOR ENERGY by Charles De Coty Marsh
This book provides for sufferers from rheumatism and allied
complaints precisely what it states – a prescription for energy.
The author's researches over the years have enabled him to be
specific on diets and menus.

THE COMPLETE RAW JUICE THERAPY by Susan E. Charmine
A most comprehensive guide to the healing and regenerative
powers of natural energy from raw juices.

A GUIDE TO THE BACH FLOWER REMEDIES by Julian Barnard
A guide to the Bach remedies (discovered in the 1930s by
Edward Bach) which are a simple and natural method of
healing through the use of certain wild flowers, the remedies
being used to treat the personality disorders of the patient
rather than the individual physical condition.

LET'S COOK IT RIGHT by Adelle Davis
A popular and helpful cookbook dedicated to the principle
that foods can be prepared to retain both flavour and nut-
rients.

Soups

Anyone who has been to France, particularly in the country areas, will have savoured the taste of a home-made soup (potage) often made while you wait. It is satisfying to know that something is made with loving care, on the premises and with fresh ingedients. Such are the soups made in all of the Cranks restaurants – never out of a tin – and made from scratch every morning.

Home-made soups are truly delicious and very easy to make, so once you have tasted them you will never want to serve the tinned variety again. Most vegetables, beans and pulses and even some fruits and nuts may be used to make soup, either chopped in a broth to give a wholesome and hearty soup, or blended in a liquidizer goblet to make a puréed soup which can then be enriched with cream.

A liquidizer is a very useful piece of equipment for producing puréed soups quickly and efficiently, but if you do not have one it is possible to achieve similar results by pressing the contents of the soup through a sieve or vegetable mill.

It is very important to remember that to make a really nourishing and well-flavoured soup you need stock, so do save every drop of vegetable water that is left over when cooking vegetables, and keep it covered in the refrigerator to use as required. If vegetable water is not available dissolve a vegetable stock cube in water as directed on the packet, or in place of the stock use Bran water or Oatmeal water (*see recipe page 49*). Some soups include milk as part of their liquid content, so for those following a non-dairy diet, plantmilk or soya milk (*see page 32*) should be used instead.

Soups are ideal for family eating, picnic or packed lunches and dinner parties. For these special occasions presentation is important and can be improved by garnishing the soup with one of the following:

chopped parsley or other fresh herbs
grated cheese
chopped nuts
small pieces of sautéed vegetable to correspond with the
    flavour of the soup

croûtons – small cubes of wholemeal bread, fried until crisp
swirl of yoghourt or fresh cream

Bran water

*This can be used as stock in soups and stews, or as part of liquid
content in bread*

Bran 3 oz (75 g)
Water 1½ pt (900 ml)

Mix bran and water together. Cover and leave to stand
overnight. Strain, cover and refrigerate. Use as required.

Makes about 1½ pt (900 ml)

Oatmeal water

Use 6 oz (175 g) fine oatmeal in place of bran. Continue as
recipe above.

Creamy onion soup

Medium-sized onions 2
Small potato 1
Butter or margarine 1 oz (25 g)
Milk 1 pt (568 ml)
Vegetable stock ½ pt (300 ml)
Bay leaf 1
Salt & pepper to taste

Chop the onion and potato. Melt the butter and sauté the
onions until transparent. Add the remaining ingredients,
bring to the boil, reduce heat and simmer, covered, for 20
minutes. Remove the bay leaf. Allow to cool slightly, then
blend in small quantities in a liquidizer goblet. Reheat to
serving temperature and adjust seasoning to taste.

Serves 4–6

Green pea soup

An economical and hearty soup, ideal for cold winter days

Green split peas 8 oz (225 g)
Water 2 pt (1.2l)
Large onion 1
Butter or margarine 2 oz (50 g)
Vegetable stock cubes 2
Salt & pepper to taste

Wash the peas well, then soak them in the measured water overnight. Chop the onion. Melt the butter in a saucepan and sauté the onion until transparent. Add stock cubes to the water. Stir until the stock cubes dissolve, then simmer for 1 hour. Season to taste. If wished, blend in a liquidizer goblet.

Serves 4–6

Cream of watercress soup

A delicately flavoured soup which can be served hot or chilled

Medium-sized onion 1
Small potato 1
Butter or margarine 1 oz (25 g)
Bunch watercress 1
Milk ½ pt (284 ml)
Vegetable stock ½ pt (300 ml)
Salt & pepper to taste
Fresh double cream 4 tbsp (60 ml)

Chop the onion and potato. Melt the butter in a saucepan and sauté the onion until transparent. Add potato, watercress, milk and stock. Bring to the boil, reduce heat, cover and simmer for 20 minutes. Allow to cool slightly then blend in small amounts in a liquidizer goblet. Return to the pan, adjust seasoning to taste, stir in the cream and reheat to serving temperature.

To serve chilled
Chill before stirring in the cream. Serve with a swirl of cream and a few sprigs of watercress to garnish.

Serves 4

Mangetout soup

Mangetout literally means 'eat all' in French – sometimes called sugar peas

Medium-sized onion 1
Mangetout (sugar peas) 8 oz (225 g)
Small potato 1
Butter or margarine 1 oz (25 g)
Vegetable stock 1 pt (600 ml)
Milk ½ pt (284 ml)
Salt & pepper to taste

Top and tail, and then wash the mangetout. Roughly chop the vegetables. Melt the butter and sauté the onion until transparent. Add the mangetout, potato and stock. Bring to the boil, reduce heat, cover and simmer for 20 minutes. Off the heat, stir in the milk. Blend the soup in a liquidizer goblet in small quantities. Return to the pan, adjust seasoning to taste and reheat to serving temperature.

To serve chilled
Chill before adding the milk. Serve with a swirl of cream.

Serves 4–6

Borscht

Originally from Russia, this soup is dramatic in colour and exciting in flavour. Serve hot or chilled

Medium-sized onion 1
Small potato 1
Raw beetroot 1 lb (450 g)
Butter or margarine 1 oz (25 g)
Vegetable stock 2 pt (1.2 l)

Cider vinegar 3 tbsp (45 ml)
Yeast extract 1 tsp (5 ml)
Salt & pepper to taste
Ground nutmeg to taste
Soured cream or natural yoghourt to garnish
Chopped parsley to garnish

Chop the vegetables. Melt the butter and sauté the onion until transparent. Add potato, beetroot and stock and bring to the boil. Reduce heat, cover and simmer for ½ hour. Allow to cool before blending in small amounts in a liquidizer goblet. Return to the saucepan, add remaining ingredients and season generously. Reheat to serving temperature. Stir in soured cream just before serving and sprinkle with chopped parsley.

To serve chilled
Blend the soup, stir in the remaining ingredients. Cover and chill until required. Garnish as above.

Serves 6

Cream of leek soup

Large leeks 2
Small potato 1
Medium-sized carrot 1
Butter or margarine 1 oz (25 g)
Vegetable stock 2 pt (1.2 l)
Salt & pepper to taste
Fresh double cream ¼ pt (142 ml)

Chop the vegetables. Melt the butter and sauté the vegetables for a few minutes, stirring occasionally. Add the stock, bring to the boil, reduce heat, cover and simmer for 20 minutes. Allow to cool slightly before blending in small amounts in a liquidizer goblet. Return to the saucepan and adjust seasoning to taste. Stir in the cream and reheat to serving temperature without boiling.

To serve chilled
Chill after blending, stir in the cream just before serving.

Serves 6

Cream of spinach & courgette soup

One of the most popular and sophisticated soups at Cranks, this is ideal for special occasions

Medium-sized onion 1
Large courgette 1
Medium-sized potato 1
Spinach 4 oz (100 g)
Oil 2 tbsp (30 ml)
Few sprigs parsley
Vegetable stock 2 pt (1.2 l)
Fresh double cream ¼ pt (142 ml)
Salt & pepper to taste

Chop the vegetables. Heat the oil in a saucepan and sauté the onion and courgette until the onion is transparent. Add potato, spinach, parsley and stock. Bring to the boil, reduce heat, cover and simmer for 20 minutes. Allow to cool before blending in small quantities in a liquidizer goblet. Return the soup to the saucepan, stir in cream and adjust seasoning to taste. Reheat gently without boiling. If wished, garnish with a swirl of fresh double cream.

Serves 4–6

Fresh tomato soup

Delicate in colour with an exciting flavour, this soup bears no resemblance to the canned varieties

Medium-sized onion 1
Small potato 1
Tomatoes 1 lb (450 g)
Butter or margarine 2 oz (50 g)

Garlic cloves 2
Bay leaf 1
Tomato paste 2 tbsp (30 ml)
Vegetable stock ¾ pt (450 ml)
Milk ¾ pt (426 ml)
Salt & pepper to taste

Chop the onion and potato. Quarter the tomatoes. Melt the butter and sauté the onion until transparent. Add potato, tomatoes, garlic, bay leaf, tomato paste and stock. Cover and simmer for 20 minutes. Off the heat, stir in the milk. Remove bay leaf. Blend in small quantities in a liquidizer goblet. Adjust seasoning to taste and reheat to serving temperature.

Serves 4–6

Apple & peanut butter soup

An unusual combination of ingredients gives this soup an original and exciting flavour

Milk 2 pt (1.2 l)
Medium-sized cooking apple 1
Peanut butter 4 tbsp (60 ml)
Lemon, juice of 1
Porridge oats 3 tbsp (45 ml)
Ground ginger ¼ tsp (1.25 ml)
Salt & pepper to taste
Chopped parsley to garnish

Heat the milk to just below boiling point. Grate the apple. Blend together the peanut butter and lemon juice, and add to the milk with remaining ingredients. Simmer for 15 minutes. Allow to cool slightly then blend in small quantities in a liquidizer goblet. Reheat to serving temperature and adjust seasoning to taste. Sprinkle with chopped parsley.
This soup may be served chilled, if wished.

Serves 6

Mushroom soup

A true favourite!

Medium-sized onion 1
Small potato 1
Mushrooms 8 oz (225 g)
Butter or margarine 2 oz (50 g)
Thyme 1 tsp (5 ml)
Large sprig parsley
Milk 1¼ pt (710 ml)
Salt & pepper to taste

Chop the vegetables. Melt the butter in a saucepan and sauté the onion until transparent. Add the potato and mushrooms and cook, stirring for 2 minutes. Add remaining ingredients, bring to the boil, reduce heat, cover and simmer for 20 minutes. Allow to cool slightly then blend in a liquidizer goblet until smooth. Reheat to serving temperature and adjust seasoning to taste.

Serves 4–6

Mulligatawny soup

A spicy, nourishing soup

Medium-sized carrot 1
Medium-sized onion 1
Medium-sized potato 1
Medium-sized cooking apple 1
Oil 2 tbsp (30 ml)
Garlic cloves, crushed 2
Curry powder 1 tbsp (15 ml)
Tomato juice ½ pt (300 ml)
Vegetable stock 2 pt (1.2 l)
Salt to taste

Chop the vegetables and apple. Heat the oil in a large saucepan and sauté the vegetables and apple until the onion is transparent. Add garlic and curry powder and cook, stirring for 2 minutes. Add all the liquids, bring to the boil, reduce heat, cover and simmer for 30 minutes. Allow to cool slightly then blend in small quantities in a liquidizer goblet. Reheat to serving temperature and adjust seasoning to taste.

Serves 6

Creamy potato soup

Medium-sized potatoes 2
Medium-sized onion 1
Oil 2 tbsp (30 ml)
Vegetable stock 1 pt (600 ml)
Milk ½ pt (284 ml)
Mixed herbs 1 tsp (5 ml)
Paprika 1 tsp (5 ml)
Caraway seeds ½ tsp (2.5 ml)
Salt & pepper to taste

Chop the vegetables. Heat the oil in a saucepan and sauté the vegetables until the onion is transparent, then add the remaining ingredients. Bring to the boil, reduce heat, cover and simmer for 20 minutes. Blend in a liquidizer goblet in small quantities. Thin with a little extra milk, if desired. Adjust seasoning to taste and reheat to serving temperature.

Serves 4–6

Carrot potage

This is based on a traditional French recipe

Carrots 1 lb (450 g)
Medium-sized potato 1
Medium-sized onion 1
Butter or margarine 1 oz (25 g)
Thyme & sage 1 tsp (5 ml) each
Vegetable stock 2 pt (1.2 l)
Yeast extract 1 tsp (5 ml)
Salt & pepper to taste

Chop the vegetables. Melt the butter, add the onion and sauté until transparent. Add the remaining ingredients, bring to the boil, reduce heat and simmer, covered, for ½ hour. Allow to cool slightly, then blend in small quantities in a liquidizer goblet until smooth. Reheat to serving temperature and adjust seasoning to taste.

Serves 4–6

Buckwheat & potato soup

A nourishing soup with a distinctive flavour

Medium-sized potato 1
Medium-sized onion 1
Vegetable stock 1½ pt (900 ml)
Buckwheat 4 oz (100 g)
Parsley, chopped 2 tbsp (30 ml)
Oregano ½ tsp (2.5 ml)
Yeast extract 1 tsp (5 ml)
Milk 1 pt (568 ml)
Soya sauce 1 tsp (5 ml)
Salt & pepper to taste

Chop the potato and onion. Bring the stock to the boil in a saucepan, then add the buckwheat, vegetables, parsley, oregano and yeast extract. Simmer, covered, for about ½ hour, until the buckwheat and vegetables are tender. After 15 minutes, check to see if the cooking liquor has been absorbed. If necessary, stir in half the milk. Allow to cool slightly, then blend in a liquidizer goblet in small quantities, adding the remaining milk as required. Add the soya sauce and seasoning, then reheat to serving temperature. Adjust seasoning to taste. Thin with extra milk or stock as necessary. If wished, top with grated cheese to serve.

Serves 4–6

Carrot, apple & cashew nut soup

Carrots 1 lb (450 g)
Large onion 1
Small potato 1
Large cooking apple 1
Butter or margarine 2 oz (50 g)
Vegetable stock 2 pt (1.2 l)
Broken cashew nuts 2 oz (50 g)
Salt & pepper to taste

Roughly chop the vegetables and apple. Melt the butter in a large saucepan and sauté the prepared vegetables for 5 minutes, stirring occasionally. Add the remaining ingredients, bring to the boil, cover and simmer for 30 minutes until the vegetables are just tender. Allow to cool before blending in a liquidizer goblet. Reheat to serving temperature and adjust seasoning to taste.

Serves 6

Armenian soup

A Marshall Street restaurant favourite, this recipe was introduced by a member of staff many years ago

Red lentils, washed 2 oz (50 g)
Dried apricots, washed 2 oz (50 g)
Large potato 1
Vegetable stock 2 pt (1.2 l)
Lemon, juice of ½
Ground cumin 1 tsp (5 ml)
Parsley, chopped 3 tbsp (45 ml)
Salt & pepper to taste

Place lentils and apricots in a large saucepan. Roughly chop the potato and add to the pan with remaining ingredients. Bring to the boil, cover and simmer for 30 minutes. Allow to cool, then blend in a liquidizer goblet until smooth. Reheat to serving temperature and adjust seasoning to taste.

Serves 4–6

Egg & lemon soup

Carrots 8 oz (225 g)
Medium-sized onion 1
Butter or margarine 1 oz (25 g)
Vegetable stock 1 pt (600 ml)
Lemon 1
Bay leaf (or ground bay leaf) 1
Milk ½ pt (284 ml)
Free-range eggs 2
Salt & pepper to taste

Chop the vegetables. Melt the butter in a large saucepan and sauté the vegetables until the onion is transparent. Add the stock, pared rind from the lemon, and bay leaf. Bring to the boil, reduce heat, cover and simmer for 25 minutes, then remove the bay leaf. Off the heat, stir in the milk, blend in a liquidizer goblet in small quantities, then return to the saucepan. Squeeze the juice from the lemon. Beat the eggs and lemon juice together and whisk them into the soup. Reheat very carefully to serving temperature. *Do not allow to boil*. Adjust seasoning to taste.

Serves 4–6

Cheddar cheese soup

Medium-sized onion 1
Medium-sized potato 1
Carrots 4 oz (100 g)
Butter or margarine 1 oz (25 g)
Vegetable stock 1 pt (600 ml)
Garlic clove, crushed 1
Thyme & sage ½ tsp (2.5 ml) each
Milk ½ pt (284 ml)
Cheddar cheese, grated 6 oz (175 g)
Salt & pepper to taste

Chop the vegetables. Melt the butter in a large saucepan and sauté the vegetables until the onion is transparent. Add the stock, garlic and herbs. Bring to the boil, reduce heat, cover and simmer for 25 minutes. Add the remaining ingredients, allow to cool slightly, then blend in a liquidizer goblet in small quantities until smooth. Reheat very carefully to serving temperature. Do not allow to boil, otherwise the cheese will go stringy. Adjust seasoning to taste.

Serves 4–6

Celery & cashew nut soup

Medium-sized onion 1
Medium-sized potato 1
Celery ½ head
Butter or margarine 1 oz (25 g)
Broken cashew nuts 3 oz (75 g)
Vegetable stock 1¼ pt (750 ml)
Milk ¾ pt (426 ml)
Salt & pepper to taste

Chop the vegetables. Melt the butter in a large saucepan and sauté the prepared vegetables gently until the onion is transparent. Add cashews and continue cooking for 5 minutes, stirring frequently. Add the stock, bring to the boil, cover and simmer for 20 minutes. Add milk, allow to cool slightly, then blend in a liquidizer goblet in small quantities. Reheat to serving temperature and adjust seasoning to taste.

Serves 4–6

Parsnip & apple soup

An unusual combination of vegetable and fruit gives this soup an exciting flavour

Butter or margarine 1 oz (25 g)
Medium-sized onion 1
Medium-sized parsnips 2
Medium-sized cooking apple 1
Vegetable stock 1 pt (600 ml)
Parsley, chopped 2 tbsp (30 ml)

Mixed herbs ½ tsp (2.5 ml)
Milk 1 pt (568 ml)
Salt & pepper to taste

Chop the vegetables. Melt the butter in a large saucepan and sauté the vegetables and apple, stirring frequently, until the onion is transparent. Add the stock and herbs, then bring to the boil and reduce heat. Cover and simmer for 30 minutes. Add the milk. Allow to cool slightly before blending in a liquidizer goblet in small quantities. Reheat to serving temperature and adjust seasoning to taste.

Serves 4–6

Cauliflower soup

A deliciously delicate flavour makes this a soup to impress guests!

Medium-sized potato 1
Medium-sized onion 1
Medium-sized cauliflower 1
Butter or margarine 1 oz (25 g)
Vegetable stock 1 pt (600 ml)
Parsley, chopped 2 tbsp (30 ml)
Ground nutmeg to taste
Milk 1 pt (568 ml)
Salt & pepper to taste

Chop the potato and onion. Melt the butter in a large saucepan and sauté the vegetables until the onion is transparent. Break the cauliflower into florets and add to the pan with the stock, parsley and nutmeg. Bring to the boil, reduce heat, cover and simmer for 20 minutes. Add the milk, allow to cool before blending in a liquidizer goblet in small quantities. Reheat to serving temperature, adjust seasoning to taste, and serve at once.

Serves 4–6

Potage Malakoff

First introduced into Marshall Street, this is now a great favourite in all Cranks restaurants

Medium-sized onion 1
Medium-sized potato 1
Large carrot 1
Large tomatoes 2
Butter or margarine 1 oz (25 g)
Few sprigs parsley
Garlic clove, crushed 1
Bay leaf 1
Vegetable stock 2 pt (1.2 l)
Soya sauce 2 tsp (10 ml)
Yeast extract 1 tsp (5 ml)
Salt & pepper to taste
Spinach, finely shredded 4 oz (100 g)

Chop the vegetables. Melt the butter in a saucepan and sauté the onion until transparent. Add the remaining ingredients, except spinach. Bring to the boil, reduce heat, cover and simmer for 30 minutes. Allow to cool before blending in small amounts in a liquidizer goblet. Return to the saucepan, add the spinach and simmer for 10 minutes. Adjust seasoning to taste.

Serves 4–6

Russian vegetable soup

Medium-sized onion 1
Medium-sized potato 1
Medium-sized parsnip 1
Carrots 4 oz (100 g)
Butter or margarine 2 oz (50 g)
Parsley, chopped 2 tbsp (30 ml)
Mixed herbs ½ tsp (2.5 ml)
Nutmeg to taste
Vegetable stock 2 pt (1.2 l)

Small leek 1
Cabbage 2oz (50 g)
Salt & pepper to taste

Chop the onion, potato, parsnip and carrots. Melt half the butter in a large saucepan and sauté the vegetables gently, stirring occasionally, until the onion is transparent. Add the parsley, herbs, nutmeg and stock and bring to the boil, reduce heat, cover and simmer for 30 minutes. Leave to cool before blending in a liquidizer goblet in small quantities. Meanwhile, finely shred the leek and cabbage and sauté them in the remaining butter until just tender. Add to the blended soup, simmer gently for 10 minutes, and adjust seasoning to taste.

Serves 4–6

Pumpkin and spinach soup

An obvious choice for Hallowe'en, but keep this recipe in mind during the short 'pumpkin season'

Medium-sized onion 1
Butter or margarine 1 oz (25 g)
Pumpkin 1 lb (450 g)
Spinach 8 oz (225 g)
Medium-sized tomatoes 2
Vegetable stock 3 pt (1.8 l)
Salt & pepper to taste

Finely chop the onion. Melt the butter in a large saucepan and sauté the onion until transparent. Dice the pumpkin, finely shred the spinach and roughly chop the tomatoes. Add vegetables to the pan with the remaining ingredients. Bring to the boil, reduce the heat, then cover and simmer for about 20 minutes until all the vegetables are tender. Adjust the seasoning to taste.

Serves 6

French onion soup

One of the great classic soups of all time. It makes a hearty meal served with wholemeal croûtons and grated cheese floating on the top

Large onions 2
Oil 3 tbsp (45 ml)
Vegetable stock 1½ pt (900 ml)
Mixed herbs 1 tsp (5 ml)
Yeast extract 1 tsp (5 ml)
Salt & pepper to taste
Wholemeal croûtons to serve
Cheddar cheese, grated 4 oz (100 g)

Finely slice the onions. Heat the oil in a saucepan and sauté the onions until golden brown. Add the remaining ingredients, bring to the boil. Reduce the heat, cover and simmer for 15 minutes. Serve with wholemeal croûtons and grated cheese.

Serves 4

Country vegetable soup

Medium-sized onion 1
Medium-sized potato 1
Small pepper 1
Medium-sized leek 1
Large courgette 1
Oil 3 tbsp (45 ml)
Vegetable stock 2 pt (1.2 l)
Tomato juice 1 pt (600 ml)
Garlic cloves, crushed 2
Bay leaf 1
Mixed herbs 1 tsp (5 ml)
Salt & pepper to taste

Chop the onion, dice the potato, cut the pepper into thin strips, shred the leek, slice the courgette. Heat the oil in a large saucepan and sauté the onion until transparent. Add the remaining vegetables and fry, stirring occasionally, for 5 minutes. Add the remaining ingredients, bring to the boil. Reduce heat, cover and simmer for about 30 minutes. Remove the bay leaf. Adjust seasoning to taste.

Serves 6

Lentil & tomato soup

A hearty and satisfying soup. Sprinkle with grated cheese and this is a meal in itself!

Small onion 1
Tomatoes 8 oz (225 g)
Oil 2 tbsp (30 ml)
Lentils 4 oz (100 g)
Tomato juice ½ pt (300 ml)
Vegetable stock 1½ pt (900 ml)
Thyme ½ tsp (2.5 ml)
Yeast extract ½ tsp (2.5 ml)
Salt & pepper to taste

Chop the onion and tomatoes. Heat the oil in a saucepan and sauté the onion until transparent. Add the remaining ingredients, cover and simmer for 30 minutes. Adjust seasoning to taste.

Serves 4–6

Chunky bean soup

Mixed dried beans 8 oz (225 g)
Large onion 1
Medium-sized carrot 1
Butter or margarine 1 oz (25 g)
Water 1½ pt (900 ml)
Garlic cloves, crushed 2
Vegetable stock cubes 2
Tomato paste 2 tbsp (30 ml)
Yeast extract 1 tsp (5 ml)
Salt & pepper to taste
Chopped parsley to garnish

Wash the beans well, soak in water overnight. Chop the onion. Dice the carrot. Melt the butter and sauté the onion until transparent. Put the drained beans into the measured water with the remaining ingredients, except the parsley. Simmer for 1 hour, or until the beans are tender. Adjust seasoning to taste. Sprinkle with parsley.

Serves 6

Hauser soup

This beautiful orange-coloured soup was created by Gaylord Hauser, the American nutritionist, and appears in his book 'Look Younger, Live Longer' – a book which was a great inspiration to the Directors in the setting up of Cranks

Large carrots 2
Small onion 1
Milk 1¾ pt (1 l)
Grated nutmeg to taste
Salt & pepper to taste
Chopped parsley to garnish

Roughly chop the vegetables. Place all the ingredients, except parsley, in a liquidizer goblet and blend until smooth. Pour into a saucepan and heat slowly to just below boiling point. Adjust seasoning to taste. Serve at once, sprinkled with chopped parsley.

This can also be served as an iced soup, made ahead and refrigerated for several hours. Place in a liquidizer goblet and blend for a few seconds, then serve sprinkled with chopped parsley.

Serves 6

Gazpacho

A delicious cold soup based on an original recipe from Andalucia

Cucumber ¼
Small green or red pepper 1
Tomatoes 8 oz (225 g)

Small onion 1
Garlic clove 1
Few sprigs parsley
Tomato juice ½ pt (300 ml)
Water ¼ pt (150 ml)
Tomato paste 1 tbsp (15 ml)
Salt & pepper to taste

Roughly chop all the vegetables. Blend all the ingredients together in small quantities in a liquidizer goblet until smooth. Chill and serve with croûtons.

Serves 4–6

Starters

Where does a 'starter' finish and a 'main course' start? The answer must be dependent on the viewpoint or mood of the cook. For in vegetarian cooking in particular a recipe used on one occasion as a main dish can, with very minor modification and in smaller quantity, be a starter for another meal.

A vegetarian wholefood regime tends to presuppose a simple mode of living, where the idea of a starter is out of place as altogether too sophisticated. But there must be occasions when having friends to a meal one is spurred on to attempt extra gastronomic delights, and a starter gives a chance to paint from a broader palette. Also, of course, on such occasions it can be helpful to give one's guests something to get on with and for conversation to develop whilst completing the preparations for the main course.

As an alternative to the usual half a grapefruit, avocado, salad or soup, this chapter introduces you to some new recipe ideas including 'pâtés' made with vegetables, cheese and even yeast, as well as hot and cold vegetable dishes and egg recipes.

Tamari cashews

These delicious roasted nuts make compulsive eating. Serve them with drinks or as a protein snack at any time

Oil 1 tbsp (15 ml)
Broken cashew nuts 1 lb (450 g)
Soya sauce 2 tbsp (30 ml)

Pour the oil into a baking tin, add the nuts and turn them in the oil. Roast in the oven at 180°C (350°F/Mark 4) for about 15 minutes, turning occasionally, until golden. Sprinkle the soya sauce over and stir the nuts until well coated. Return to the oven for 5 minutes. Stir again and leave to cool in the tin. Store in an airtight container.

Hummus

A tangy dip popular in Greek and Turkish restaurants. Make it at home and you can vary the flavour of lemon and garlic to suit particular taste

Chick peas, soaked overnight 8 oz (225 g)
Water
Garlic cloves 2
Oil 3 tbsp (45 ml)
Lemons, juice of 1–2
Natural yoghourt 4 tbsp (60 ml)
Salt & pepper to taste
Chopped parsley to garnish
Paprika to garnish

Place the chick peas in a saucepan, and just cover with water. Add the garlic cloves. Bring to the boil, cover and simmer for 30 minutes, adding extra water if necessary. Allow to cool in the water. Put oil, juice of 1 lemon and yoghourt into a liquidizer goblet, add half the chick peas with the cooking liquid and the garlic, and blend until smooth. Keep adding chick peas and extra water if necessary, until they have all been incorporated. Season with salt and pepper, adding extra lemon juice if wished. Transfer to a serving dish, sprinkle with chopped parsley and paprika, and serve with wholemeal bread or melba toast.

Serves 6

Garlic relish

The Cranks variation of a translated French recipe

Wholemeal breadcrumbs 4 oz (100 g)
Hot water ¼ pt (150 ml)
Large onion 1
Butter or margarine 2 oz (50 g)
Fresh yeast 1 oz (25 g)
Garlic cloves, crushed 2–3
Thyme 1 tbsp (15 ml)
Salt & pepper to taste

Soak the breadcrumbs in hot water. Finely chop the onion. Melt the butter in a saucepan and sauté the onion until transparent. Add the soaked bread and any excess liquid and cook over high heat, stirring all the time until no free liquid remains. Off the heat, crumble in the yeast and add the remaining ingredients. Adjust seasoning. Beat well and press into a shallow serving dish. Cover and leave to cool. Serve on individual plates with a salad garnish and triangles of wholemeal toast.

This can also be used as a spread or sandwich filling.

Serves 6

Mushroom pâté

A variation of Garlic relish, and equally as good

Medium-sized onion 1
Mushrooms 1 lb (450 g)
Butter or margarine 2 oz (50 g)
Wholemeal breadcrumbs 6 oz (175 g)
Hot water ¼ pt (150 ml)
Lemon, juice of ½
Garlic cloves, crushed (optional) 1–2
Fresh yeast, crumbled 1 oz (25 g)
Ground nutmeg to taste
Salt & pepper to taste

Finely chop the onion, mushroom caps and stalks. Melt the butter in a saucepan and sauté the onion until transparent. Add the mushrooms and cook for a further 2–3 minutes. Soak the breadcrumbs in the hot water, then add to the mushrooms with the lemon juice and garlic. Cook over gentle heat until no free liquid remains. Off the heat, beat in the remaining ingredients and check seasoning to taste. Spoon into a serving dish, cover and refrigerate until required. Garnish with raw mushroom slices.

This can also be used as a spread or sandwich filling.

Serves 6

Cream cheese & cashew nut pâté

Small carrot 1
Cream cheese 8 oz (225 g)

Broken cashew nuts, roasted & ground 4 oz (100 g)
Chopped parsley 1 tbsp (15 ml)
Salt & pepper to taste
Parsley to garnish

Finely grate the carrot. Beat all the ingredients together in a basin. Press the mixture into individual ramekin dishes, cover and refrigerate until required. Garnish with parsley sprigs and slices of raw carrot. Serve with toast.

This can also be used as a spread or sandwich filling.

Serves 4–6

Wine & nut pâté

This pâté was first introduced into our 'Dine & Wine' evenings. It's a very special recipe and needs weighing out accurately. Ideal for entertaining, as it can be made a day or two before it is needed

Onion, small 1
Celery sticks 2
Butter or margarine ½ oz (15 g)
Ground cumin 1 tsp (5 ml)
Paprika 1 tsp (5 ml)
Basil 1 tsp (5 ml)
Vegetable stock or water ¼ pt (150 ml)
Red wine ¼ pt (150 ml)
*Cooked chestnuts, ground 4 oz (100 g)
Shelled walnuts, ground 4 oz (100 g)
Shelled pecans, ground 4 oz (100 g)
Wholemeal breadcrumbs 2 oz (50 g)
Chopped parsley 4 tbsp (60 ml)
Garlic clove, crushed 1
Soya sauce 1 tbsp (15 ml)
Brandy 1 tbsp (15 ml)
Free-range eggs 2
Salt & pepper to taste

Grease and line the base of a 2 lb (900 g) loaf tin. Skin and finely chop the onion. Trim and finely chop the celery. Melt the butter in a saucepan and sauté the vegetables until soft.

Add the spices and herbs and cook, stirring for 1 minute. Add the vegetable stock and wine and bring to the boil. Off the heat, stir in the nuts, breadcrumbs, parsley, garlic, soya sauce, and brandy. Mix well, then add the beaten eggs and season generously.

Spoon the mixture into the prepared tin and level the surface. Bake in the oven at 180°C (350°F/Mark 4) for about 40 minutes until slightly firm to the touch. Leave to go cold in the tin, then turn out on to a plate. Serve in slices.

For a decorative finish make up ¼ pt (150 ml) agar-agar following the instructions on the packet. Brush the top and sides of the pâté with agar-agar and arrange lemon slices along its length. Brush a second time with agar-agar to glaze the loaf completely.

*Use fresh chestnuts where possible. Make a nick in 6 oz (175 g) chestnuts to pierce the skins. Bring to the boil in water, cover and simmer for 30 minutes. Cool and remove the skins. Alternatively, use 4 oz (100 g) canned chestnuts.

Serves 6–8

Egg & tomato mousse

Free-range eggs, hard-boiled & shelled 6
Medium-sized tomatoes 2
Small green pepper ½
Milk 2 tbsp (30 ml)
Mayonnaise (*see page 103*) 3 tbsp (45 ml)
Salt & pepper to taste
Agar-agar 2 tsp (10 ml)
Water ¼ pt (150 ml)
Tomato slices to garnish

Roughly chop the eggs, quarter the tomatoes, and chop the pepper. Place them in a liquidizer goblet with the milk and mayonnaise. Blend until smooth. Season generously. Dissolve the agar-agar in the water according to the instructions on the label. Off the heat, beat some of the egg mixture into the agar-agar, then return this mixture to the bulk. Stir well to mix evenly, then spoon into a serving dish or individual dishes. Cover and refrigerate until required. Garnish with tomato slices. Serve with toast.

Serves 6

Baked grapefruit – I

This is good at breakfast time or as a pudding

Grapefruit 2
Clear honey 4 tsp (20 ml)
Ground cinnamon (optional)

Cut the grapefruit in half. Remove the central pith with a grapefruit knife, then loosen the segments. Pour honey into the centre of each grapefruit half and sprinkle with cinnamon, if wished. Bake in the oven at 190°C (375°F/Mark 5) for about 15 minutes. Serve warm.

Serves 4

Baked grapefruit – II

Grapefruit 2
Raw brown sugar 4 tsp (20 ml)
Butter or margarine 1 oz (25 g)
Ground cinnamon 1 tsp (5 ml)

Cut the grapefruit in half. Remove the central pith with a grapefruit knife, then loosen the segments. Mix together the sugar, butter and cinnamon and spread over the fruit. Bake in the oven at 190°C (375°F/Mark 5) for about 15 minutes. Serve warm.

Serves 4

Florida salad

This is also ideal for breakfast or as a dessert

Medium-sized grapefruit 2
Medium-sized oranges 2
Clear honey 2 tbsp (30 ml)

Peel the grapefruit and oranges, removing all the white pith. Using a sharp knife 'free' the fruit segments from the membrane. Squeeze out any excess juice and reserve. Arrange the segments in a serving dish. Mix the honey and fruit juice together and pour over the fruit. Cover and leave in a cool place to marinate.

Serves 4

Mushrooms à la grecque

Water ¼ pt (150 ml)
Garlic cloves, finely chopped 2
Lemons, juice of 2
Olive oil 2 tbsp (30 ml)
Salt & pepper to taste
Bay leaf 1
Sprig of parsley 1
Button mushrooms 12 oz (350 g)
Large tomato 1
Chopped parsley to garnish

Put the first 7 ingredients into a saucepan. Bring to the boil and boil for 5 minutes. Add the mushrooms and simmer, covered, for a further 5 minutes. Add the chopped tomato, then refrigerate until really cold. Sprinkle with chopped parsley before serving.

This can also be served as a salad.

Serves 4–6

Ratatouille

This speciality from Provence is good served hot or cold

Medium-sized onion 1
Large red or green pepper 1
Large aubergine 1
Large courgettes 2
Oil 4 tbsp (60 ml)
Tomatoes 6

Garlic cloves, crushed 2–3
Oregano ½ tsp (2.5 ml)
Basil ½ tsp (2.5 ml)
Tomato juice ¾ pt (450 ml)
Salt & pepper to taste

Chop the onion and pepper, dice the aubergine and slice the courgettes. Heat the oil in a large saucepan, add the onion and aubergine and sauté until the onion is transparent. Add the courgettes and pepper and sauté for a further 5 minutes, stirring occasionally. Add the remaining ingredients and simmer, covered, for 15–20 minutes. Serve hot or cold.

Serves 4–6

Stuffed tomatoes

A summer special suitable for picnics and parties

Medium-sized firm tomatoes 6
Fresh wholemeal breadcrumbs 4 oz (100 g)
Cream cheese 4 oz (100 g)
Spring onion or chives, chopped 2 tbsp (30 ml)
Salt & pepper to taste
Parsley sprigs to garnish

Wash and dry the tomatoes. Cut a 'lid' off the top of each and scoop out and chop the pulp. Leave the tomato shells upside down on kitchen paper to drain. Add breadcrumbs, cream cheese and onion to the tomato pulp and beat well. Season to taste. Fill the tomatoes with the cheese mixture, replace the lids and garnish each with a sprig of parsley. Refrigerate until required.

Makes 6

Creamy baked tomatoes

Very large tomatoes 4
Salt & pepper to taste
Basil 1 tsp (5 ml)

Fresh double cream 4 tbsp (60 ml)
Cheddar cheese, grated 2 oz (50 g) or **Parmesan, grated 1 oz (25 g)**

Halve the tomatoes and place in individual ovenproof dishes. Sprinkle generously with salt, pepper and basil. Bake in the oven at 200°C (400°F/Mark 6), for 10 minutes. Spoon the cream over and sprinkle with cheese. Return to the oven for a further 10 minutes. Serve at once.

Serves 4

Tarragon eggs en cocotte

To make a tasty main meal, double the quantity of ingredients and bake in one large, shallow, ovenproof dish

Small onion 1
Tomatoes 8 oz (225 g)
Butter or margarine 1 oz (25 g)
Tarragon 1 tsp (5 ml)
Salt & pepper to taste
Free-range eggs 4
Fresh double cream 4 tbsp (60 ml)

Finely chop the onion and the tomatoes. Melt the butter in a saucepan and sauté the onion until transparent. Add the tomatoes and tarragon and cook over gentle heat, stirring frequently until soft and pulpy. Adjust seasoning to taste. Spoon the mixture into 4 individual ovenproof dishes. Make a 'well' in the centre and break an egg into each one. Spoon the cream over and bake in the oven at 200°C (400°F/Mark 6) for 10–15 minutes, according to taste. Serve at once.

Serves 4

Eggs Indienne

An interesting variation of stuffed eggs – good for party food

Small onion 1
Large tomato 1

Butter or margarine 1 oz (25 g)
Curry powder 1 tsp (5 ml)
Sultanas 1 tbsp (15 ml)
Lemon juice to taste
Salt to taste
Free-range eggs, hard-boiled & shelled 6
Sprigs of parsley to garnish

Finely chop the onion and the tomato. Melt the butter in a saucepan and sauté the onion until transparent. Stir in the curry powder and cook for 1–2 minutes. Add the tomato, sultanas and a squeeze of lemon juice and cook, stirring until soft and pulpy. Allow to cool. Cut the eggs in half lengthways, scoop out the yolks and rub them through a sieve. Mix the yolks with the curry mixture, then spoon the mixture into the halved eggs. Garnish with sprigs of parsley.

Serves 4–6

Egg mayonnaise

Small lettuce, finely shredded 1
Free-range eggs, hard-boiled & shelled 4
Mayonnaise (*see page 103*) ¼ pt (150 ml)
Paprika to garnish

Arrange a bed of shredded lettuce on 1 large or 4 individual plates. Cut eggs in half lengthwise and arrange cut-side down on the lettuce. Coat with mayonnaise (thinned with a little milk, if necessary) and sprinkle with paprika.

Serves 4

Nut 'cheese' (*vegan*)

Cranks own version of a vegan substitute for dairy cheese

Margarine 4 oz (100 g)
Mixed nuts, finely ground 6 oz (175 g)
Yeast extract 1 tsp (5 ml)

Melt the margarine over gentle heat. Stir in the ground nuts and yeast extract. Pour the 'cheese' into a container, cover and refrigerate until set. Serve with wholemeal toast.

Serves 4–6

Sava *(vegan)*

A soya-based alternative to dairy cheese. Try the variations listed below, then experiment with other flavours.

Margarine 4 oz (100 g)
Soya flour 4 oz (100 g)
Garlic clove, crushed 1
Yeast extract 1 tsp (5 ml)

Melt the margarine in a saucepan over gentle heat. Stir in the soya flour and cook, stirring for a few minutes until slightly thickened. Off the heat, stir in the garlic and yeast extract. Pour into a container, cover and chill until set.

VARIATIONS
Curry Stir in 1 tsp (5 ml) curry powder with the soya flour.

Tomato Stir in 1–2 tbsp (15–30 ml) tomato paste. Omit garlic.

Herb Add freshly chopped herbs to taste.

Soya curd 'cheese' *(vegan)*

A soya-based alternative to dairy cheese made by the traditional method

Soya flour 4 oz (100 g)
Water 1 pt (600 ml)
Lemons, juice of 2
Salt & pepper to taste

Mix the soya flour to a paste with some of the water. Bring the remaining water to the boil, pour on to the soya paste, then return to the saucepan. Bring to the boil, stirring continuously, then simmer for 5 minutes. Off the heat, stir in the lemon juice and leave to cool. Place some wetted muslin in a large sieve, over a basin. Pour the contents of the saucepan on to the muslin and leave until all the liquid has drained through, producing a firm 'curd'. Adjust seasoning to taste. For added flavour, stir in chopped herbs or crushed garlic.

Serves 4–6

Salads

Salads are as good, or as bad, as their basic ingredients, so it is always important to start off with good quality vegetables and fruit. How often one has seen limp lettuce leaves arranged on a plate with a few slices of cucumber and tomato and been told that it is a salad. A salad should be a delightful combination of flavours, colour and texture. This is achieved by carefully considering the ingredients and producing a well-balanced mixture. For example, crisp beanshoots combine extremely well with the soft, sweet texture of sliced banana and the richness of roasted peanuts; when tossed in a slightly spicy ginger dressing, they make a perfect salad.

Cranks produce a selection of salads every morning, which are sold in the restaurants and as 'take-aways'. The combination of ingredients will vary with the seasons. In winter raw, grated root vegetables, cooked or sprouted beans and rice or pasta are among the most popular bases. In summer there is a wealth of choice among the more delicate leaf vegetables and typical salad ingredients.

The combination of ingredients is almost limitless when it comes to making salad, as most vegetables and fruits combine well and complement each other. Nuts, seeds, dried fruit and herbs can all add extra flavour and texture. It is also true that too many ingredients can spoil a salad mixture; it is necessary to be able to taste the individual ingredients that go to make up the salad.

If you are making a selection of salads at home, always start with a variety of basic ingredients. For example, potato, shredded red cabbage, green leaves and a fruit such as apple or orange would constitute a good cross-section, in terms of colour and texture. Preparation of the ingredients is important. A lot of the goodness in fruit and vegetables lies in or just below the skin, so wash, scrub and trim them as necessary, but never peel unless absolutely essential. This is a general principle in the preparation of all fruit and vegetables and cannot be over-emphasized.

Having prepared the salad, the next stage is to 'dress' it. This involves tossing the salad in a dressing, which may be a thick, creamy one, such as mayonnaise, or a thinner one such as French dressing. Whichever one you choose, it is important to coat the salad ingredients well with the dressing, but not to swamp the salad in too much liquid.

TO TOSS A SALAD

A tossed salad should be one in which the ingredients are just coated with dressing so that they glisten. There should not be an excess of dressing in the bottom of the salad bowl. To do this, place the salad in a large bowl, pour a little dressing over the salad, and using salad servers or two spoons, carefully turn the salad ingredients in a rotating movement until evenly coated. Add a little more dressing if necessary and repeat.

As a general rule, green leaf salads should be tossed just before serving. Root vegetable salads, marinated salads and those tossed in mayonnaise will improve if dressed the day before, and will keep in a refrigerator for two or three days. The exceptions to this include watery vegetables, particularly tomatoes, which lose their flavour if kept for more than 24 hours.

Carrot mayonnaise

A colourful salad which may be kept for a few days in the refrigerator

Carrots 1 lb (450 g)
Mayonnaise (*see page 103*) ¼ pt (150 ml)
Sunflower seeds 1 oz (25 g)
Chopped parsley 4 tbsp (60 ml)
Salt & pepper to taste

Finely grate the carrots, stir in the mayonnaise, sunflower seeds and parsley. Season to taste. Cover and chill until required.

Serves 4–6

Coleslaw

The translation of coleslaw is cabbage salad, but it is far more interesting than its name suggests. This is the most popular combination of ingredients, but experiment with others to make new variations

White cabbage 12 oz (350 g)
Carrots 8 oz (225 g)
Small onion 1
Mayonnaise (*see page 103*) ½ pt (300 ml)
Caraway seeds ½ tsp (2.5 ml)

Shred the cabbage, grate the carrot and finely chop the onion. Combine all the ingredients together in a mixing bowl. Toss well. Cover and chill until required.

This will keep for several days in a refrigerator.

Serves 6

Cucumber in tarragon dressing

The delicate flavours of cucumber and tarragon complement each other very successfully to make this a refreshing salad

French dressing (*see page 102*) 4 tbsp (60 ml)
Tarragon, chopped ½ tsp (2.5 ml)
Cucumber 1
Salt & pepper to taste

Combine the dressing and tarragon in a mixing bowl. Score along the length of the cucumber with a fork. Dice the cucumber and toss in the dressing. Adjust seasoning to taste. Cover and chill until required.

This will keep for 2–3 days in a refrigerator.

Serves 4–6

Waldorf salad

This is a 'winner' at the latest Cranks branch in Covent Garden Market

Celery sticks 4
Walnuts 2 oz (50 g)
Large dessert apple 1
Cheddar cheese 6 oz (175 g)

Mayonnaise (*see page 103*) ¼ pt (150 ml)
Salt & pepper to taste

Chop the celery and walnuts. Dice the apple and cheese. Mix all the ingredients together in a salad bowl. Adjust seasoning to taste.

Serves 4–6

Spinach & mushroom salad

Wholemeal bread 4 oz (100 g)
Garlic cloves, chopped 2
Oil ¼ pt (150 ml)
Fresh spinach 8 oz (225 g)
Button mushrooms 4 oz (100 g)
French dressing (*see page 102*) 6 tbsp (90 ml)
Lemon, grated rind of ½
Salt & pepper to taste

Cut the bread into ½″ (1.5 cm) cubes. Heat the garlic and oil together in a frying pan. Remove the garlic when it has browned, and fry the bread cubes until crisp and golden. Drain on absorbent kitchen paper and leave until cold. Shred the spinach into small pieces, slice the mushrooms. Put spinach, mushrooms and croûtons in a salad bowl. Mix the dressing and lemon rind and toss the salad. Adjust seasoning and serve at once.

Serves 4–6

Beetroot, celery & orange salad

Raw beetroot 8 oz (225 g)
Celery sticks, trimmed 2
Small orange, grated rind & juice of 1
French dressing (*see page 102*) 3 tbsp (45 ml)
Garlic clove, crushed 1

Grate the beetroot and chop the celery. Put the beetroot and celery in a salad bowl. Combine the orange rind and juice,

French dressing and garlic. Pour over vegetables and toss well. Cover and chill until required.

This will keep for 2–3 days in a refrigerator.

Serves 4–6

Potato salad

Potatoes 2 lb (900 g)
Small onion 1
French dressing (*see page 102*) ¼ pt (150 ml)
Chopped parsley 4 tbsp (60 ml)
Salt & pepper to taste

Cut up the potatoes (if using small new potatoes, leave whole) and steam for about 20 minutes until just tender, then dice. Finely chop the onion. Place the potatoes and onion in a bowl and pour over the dressing whilst still warm. Toss well. Cover and chill until required. Stir in the parsley before serving, and adjust seasoning to taste.

This will keep for several days in a refrigerator.

Serves 6

Carrot & swede in soured cream dressing

Raw carrots are always popular in salads, but this unusual combination of root vegetables is surprisingly good

Swede 8 oz (225 g)
Carrots 8 oz (225 g)
Soured cream dressing (*see page 103*) 1 quantity

Finely grate the swede and carrot. Combine the ingredients together in a mixing bowl and toss well. Cover and chill until required.

Serves 4–6

Celery & apple salad

A really crunchy salad with an unusual dressing

Celery, head of 1
Dessert apples 2
Honey & lemon dressing (*see page 105*) 1 quantity
Salt & pepper to taste

Slice the celery and apples. Combine all the ingredients together and toss well. Adjust seasoning to taste.

Serves 4–6

Wholewheat mayonnaise

A substantial and nutritious salad which may be made in advance and kept in the refrigerator for a few days

Wholewheat 8 oz (225 g)
Carrots 4 oz (100 g)
Small onion ½
Mayonnaise (*see page 103*) ¼ pt (150 ml)
Salt & pepper to taste

Cook the wheat in boiling water until just tender (30–45 minutes, depending on taste). Drain and leave to cool. Grate the carrots, finely chop the onion. Mix all the ingredients together and toss well. Adjust seasoning to taste. Cover and chill until required.

Cooking time may be reduced by soaking the wheat, preferably overnight.

Serves 6

Hawaiian rice salad

An exciting combination of flavour and texture

Long-grain brown rice 4 oz (100 g)
French dressing (*see page 102*) 4 tbsp (60 ml)
Small pineapple ½
Medium-sized green pepper ½
Salt & pepper to taste

Cook the rice in boiling water until tender – about 35 minutes. Drain and allow to cool, then toss in the French dressing. Cut the flesh from the pineapple and dice it. Chop the green pepper and add to the rice with the pineapple. Adjust the seasoning to taste.

Serves 4

Creamy beetroot salad

Raw beetroot 8 oz (225 g)
Parsnip 8 oz (225 g)
Chopped parsley 3 tbsp (45 ml)
Soured cream ¼ pt (142 ml)
Cider vinegar 2 tbsp (30 ml)
Salt & pepper to taste

Grate the beetroot and parsnip together, and add the parsley. Combine the remaining ingredients, then mix together with the vegetables. Toss well.

Serves 6

Leek salad

Leeks are an unusual vegetable to use in a salad, but very quick to prepare and combined with the other ingredients make a very colourful salad

Large leeks, well trimmed 2
Small red pepper 1
Walnuts, chopped 1 oz (25 g)
Lemon, grated rind & juice of 1
Mayonnaise or French dressing (*see pages 103 or 102*)
**   6 tbsp (90 ml)**
Salt & pepper to taste

Very finely shred the leeks, then blanch them in boiling water for 2 minutes, drain and cool. Slice the red pepper. Put the leeks, pepper and walnuts in a salad bowl. Mix the lemon rind and juice with the mayonnaise and toss the salad. Adjust seasoning to taste.

Serves 4–6

Italian pasta salad

Wholemeal pasta rings 4 oz (100 g)
Medium-sized red pepper 1
Black olives 2 oz (50 g)
Chopped parsley 3 tbsp (45 ml)
French dressing (*see page 102*) 4 tbsp (60 ml)
Garlic clove, crushed 1
Salt & pepper to taste

Cook the pasta rings in boiling water for about 15 minutes
until just tender. Drain and rinse in cold water. Dice the red
pepper and place in a salad bowl with the pasta, olives and
parsley. Mix the French dressing with the garlic and pour over
the salad. Toss well. Adjust seasoning to taste.

If pasta rings are not available, use any other small pasta
shape, such as broken macaroni.

Serves 4–6

Bulghur salad

Bulghur wheat makes a light but substantial base to this salad

Bulghur wheat 8 oz (225 g)
Small green pepper 1
Spring onions, chopped 2 tbsp (30 ml)
Chopped parsley 3 tbsp (45 ml)
Soya sauce 3 tbsp (45 ml)
French dressing (*see page 102*) 6 tbsp (90 ml)
Salt & pepper to taste

Place the bulghur wheat in a mixing bowl and pour ¾ pt (450
ml) boiling water over it. Fork through from time to time and
leave to cool. Chop the green pepper. Fluff up the bulghur
with a fork, then add the remaining ingredients and mix well.
Adjust seasoning to taste. Cover and chill until required.

Serves 6

Celery, cucumber & grape salad

Celery sticks 4
Cucumber ½
Red grapes 8 oz (225 g)

Dressing
Natural yoghourt ¼ pt (142 ml)
Honey 1 tsp (5 ml)
French mustard 1 tsp (5 ml)
Salt & pepper to taste

Chop the celery, slice the cucumber, halve the grapes and remove pips. Put all the salad ingredients together in a bowl. Mix together the ingredients for the dressing and season well with salt and pepper. Pour over the salad and toss.

Serves 4–6

Cauliflower, date & banana salad

The crunchy texture of cauliflower combined with the delicate fruit flavours in a tangy dressing produces a delightful salad – good on its own or as part of a salad selection

Cauliflower 1
Dates, stoned 2 oz (50 g)
Bananas 2
Mayonnaise (*see page 103*) ¼ pt (150 ml)
Lemon, grated rind & juice of 1

Break the cauliflower into florets, then steam for 5 minutes. Cool quickly. Chop the dates and slice the bananas. Mix the mayonnaise, lemon rind and juice together. Combine all the ingredients in a salad bowl and serve.

Serves 4–6

Green pepper & orange salad

A perfect summer salad, both colourful and refreshing. For a special occasion arrange the tossed salad on a bed of lettuce and garnish with sprigs of fresh mint

Medium-sized green peppers 2
Large oranges 2
Small onion 1
French dressing (*see page 102*) 4 tbsp (60 ml)

Shred the peppers, peel the oranges, remove the white pith and chop the flesh. Cut the onion into thin rings. Combine all the ingredients in a bowl. Toss well, cover and chill until required.

Serves 4–6

Alfalfa salad

Sprouted alfalfa (*see page 26*) 8 oz (225 g)
Box mustard & cress 1
Creamy paprika dressing (*see page 104*) 6 tbsp (90 ml)

Mix the alfalfa and mustard and cress together. Just before serving toss in the dressing.

Serves 4

Taboullah

Originating in the Middle East, this salad is best made with fresh mint to bring out its full flavour

Cracked wheat 8 oz (225 g)
Medium-sized onion 1
Fresh mint, chopped (or dried mint) 1 tbsp (15 ml)
Chopped parsley 6 tbsp (90 ml)
Piquant dressing (*see page 104*) ¼ pt (150 ml)

Place the cracked wheat in a basin and pour over sufficient boiling water to cover. Leave to soak for ½ hour. Drain and rinse well. Finely chop the onion. Combine all the ingredients together and toss well into the dressing. Cover and chill until required.

This will keep for several days in a refrigerator.

Serves 6

Chicory & oranges with cheese dressing

Medium heads of chicory 2
Medium-sized oranges 3
Chopped parsley to garnish

Dressing
French dressing (*see page 102*) 2 tbsp (30 ml)
Skimmed milk soft cheese 4 tbsp (60 ml)

Cut the bottom half of each head of chicory into slices and separate the top half into its individual leaves. Peel the oranges, remove any white pith and slice thinly. Reserve any juice. Combine all the chicory and orange in a bowl. Sprinkle with parsley. Using a fork, mix together the French dressing and soft cheese until smooth, then stir in the orange juice. Pour over the salad and serve at once.

Serves 4–6

Green bean salad

Green haricot beans 1 lb (450 g)
Piquant dressing (*see page 104*) ¼ pt (150 ml)
Tomatoes 8 oz (225 g)

Top and tail the beans. Steam for about 20 minutes until just tender. While the beans are still warm, pour the dressing over them. Chop the tomatoes and add to the beans. Cover and leave to cool. Chill until required.

VARIATION
Bobby beans can be used instead in this recipe. They are more rounded than the young green haricot beans and would need to be cut into bite-sized pieces before the dressing is added.

Serves 4–6

Green salad

Green salad is served every day in Cranks restaurants. To vary the salad use an equal quantity of spinach, curly endive or other green leaf salad vegetable to replace the lettuce

Medium lettuce 1
Small onion 1
Box of mustard & cress 1
French dressing (*see page 102*)

Wash, dry and shred the lettuce. Cut the onion into fine rings. Place the salad ingredients in a large bowl. Toss well with sufficient French dressing to coat.

Serves 4–6

Flageolet bean salad

Delicate shades of green make this a most attractive salad, best made in advance to allow the flavours to blend

Flageolet beans, soaked overnight 8 oz (225 g)
Lemon, grated rind & juice of 1
Oil 4 tbsp (60 ml)
Garlic clove, crushed 1
Chopped parsley 3 tbsp (45 ml)
Salt & pepper to taste

Cook the beans in boiling water for about 1 hour, or until just tender, drain well. Combine the remaining ingredients and pour over the beans. Cover and leave to marinate for several hours. Adjust seasoning to taste.

Serves 4

Tomato salad

For this salad choose firm, good quality tomatoes and cut them with a serrated knife to give even slices. This recipe is ideal as a starter served with chunks of warm wholemeal bread

Tomatoes 1 lb (450 g)
Small onion 1
Chopped parsley 2 tbsp (30 ml)
French dressing (*see page 102*) 4 tbsp (60 ml)

Thinly slice the tomatoes. Cut the onion into fine rings. Arrange them both on a platter. Sprinkle with chopped parsley and dressing. Cover and chill until required.

Serves 4

Beanshoot salad

Beanshoots have become very popular in the last few years. They are available in many supermarkets, but can be easily sprouted at home for very little cost (see page 26)

Whole peanuts 2 oz (50 g)
Oil 1 tsp (5 ml)
Salt ½ tsp (2.5 ml)
Carrots 2 oz (50 g)
Bananas 2
Fresh beanshoots 8 oz (225 g)
Creamy paprika dressing (*see page 104*)

Put the peanuts, oil and salt in a small ovenproof dish. Mix well, then roast in the oven at 200°C (400°F/Mark 6) for about 10 minutes, until golden. Leave until cold. Grate the carrots and slice the bananas. Combine with the peanuts and beanshoots. Toss in sufficient dressing to moisten.

Serves 4–6

Cabbage & orange salad

White cabbage 12 oz (350 g)
Oranges 3
Sunflower seeds 2 oz (50 g)
Chopped parsley 4 tbsp (60 ml)
Natural yoghourt ¼ pt (142 ml)
Salt & pepper to taste

Finely shred the cabbage. Peel the oranges, remove all the white pith, then cut the orange segments away from the membrane. Combine the cabbage, orange segments and remaining ingredients. Toss well.

Serves 6

Cucumber, tomato & cheese salad

Large tomatoes 3
Large cucumber ½
White Cheshire cheese 4 oz (100 g)
French dressing (*see page 102*) 4 tbsp (60 ml)

Chop the tomatoes and dice the cucumber and cheese. Combine all ingredients together in a bowl and toss well.

Serves 4

Watercress & carrot salad

Everyday ingredients which combine well to give a colourful and light textured salad

Bunch of watercress 1
Carrots 8 oz (225 g)
French dressing (*see page 102*) 3 tbsp (45 ml)

Wash the watercress and remove any coarse stems. Coarsely grate the carrots. Combine all the ingredients and toss well. Serve at once.

Serves 4

Avocado salad

This speciality salad should be arranged on individual plates to serve as a starter or side salad

Ripe avocado pears 2
Large tomatoes 2
Small onion ½
French dressing (*see page 102*) 6 tbsp (90 ml)
Chopped parsley 2 tbsp (30 ml)

Halve the avocado pears and remove the stones. Peel and slice them, then arrange in a shallow dish. Finely chop the tomatoes and onion and combine with remaining ingredients and pour over the avocado pears. Serve at once.

Serves 4–6

Sweet & sour radishes

An unusual method of preparing radishes which gives them a piquant flavour. Serve them as part of a selection of salads

Bunch of radishes 1
Salt 1 tsp (5 ml)
Soya sauce 2 tsp (10 ml)
Cider vinegar 2 tbsp (30 ml)
Raw brown sugar 2 tbsp (30 ml)
Sesame oil 1 tsp (5 ml)

Trim the radishes, then 'scratch' the surface with the prongs of a fork. Place in a single layer on a plate and sprinkle with the salt. Leave for 10 minutes. Wash and dry the radishes on kitchen paper. Combine the remaining ingredients and pour over the radishes. Cover and leave to marinate for several hours.

Serves 4

Lentil sprout salad

Lentil sprouts (*see page 26*) 12 oz (350 g)
French dressing (*see page 102*) 4 tbsp (60 ml)
Ground ginger 1 tsp (5 ml)
Large grapefruit 2
Cashew nuts, roasted 2 oz (50 g)
Salt to taste

Put the lentil sprouts in a bowl. Mix the French dressing and ground ginger and pour over the lentil sprouts. Peel the grapefruit, remove all the white pith and loosen the segments from the membrane. Add to the salad with their juice. Add cashew nuts and season to taste with salt.

Serves 6

Spiced pepper salad

This can be made in advance and kept for several days in the refrigerator

Medium-sized red peppers 2
Medium-sized onion 1
Pickling spice 1 tbsp (15 ml)
Mushrooms 4 oz (100 g)
French dressing (*see page 102*) ¼ pt (150 ml)

Slice the peppers and onion. Tie the pickling spice in a small piece of muslin. Place the vegetables in a basin with the pickling spice and pour boiling water over. Leave to stand for 10 minutes, then drain. Slice and add the mushrooms. Bring the French dressing to the boil and pour over. Cover and leave to marinate. Remove the pickling spice before serving.

Serves 4–6

Turmeric rice salad

Long-grain brown rice 6 oz (175 g)
Sultanas 3 oz (75 g)
Turmeric ½ tsp (2.5 ml)
Garlic clove, crushed 1
French dressing (*see page 102*) 4 tbsp (60 ml)
Salt & pepper to taste
Chopped parsley to garnish

Cook the rice in boiling water for 30–35 minutes until just tender. Drain. Combine the sultanas, turmeric, garlic and French dressing. Pour over the rice and stir well. Cover and refrigerate until required. Fork through, adjust seasoning to taste and sprinkle with chopped parsley before serving.

Serves 4

Ploughman's salad

This recipe was created as a main meal salad to serve at Cranks in Covent Garden Market and has become a much requested favourite

Cheddar cheese 8 oz (225 g)
Green eating apples 3
Onion, finely-chopped 1 tbsp (15 ml)
Parsley, chopped 2 tbsp (30 ml)

Natural yoghourt 4 tbsp (60 ml)
French dressing (*see page 102*) 4 tbsp (60 ml)

Finely dice the cheese, remove the core and dice the apples.
Put the cheese, apples, onion and parsley in a mixing bowl.
Whisk together the natural yoghourt and French dressing
until evenly mixed, then pour over the salad. Mix well.

Serves 4–6

Tangy courgette salad

Small courgettes 1 lb (450 g)
Lemon, grated rind & juice of 1
Garlic clove, crushed 1
Oil 3 tbsp (45 ml)
Salt & pepper to taste

Thinly slice the courgettes. Pour boiling water over and leave
for 5 minutes. Drain. Combine the remaining ingredients and
pour over the courgettes. Adjust seasoning tste. Cover and
leave to cool.

Serves 4

Tzatziki salad

A salad with a cool refreshing flavour

Cucumber 1
Garlic cloves 2
Natural yoghourt ½ pt (284 ml)
Fresh mint, chopped 1 tbsp (15 ml)
Parsley, chopped 1 tbsp (15 ml)
Salt to taste
Paprika to taste

Dice the cucumber and crush the garlic cloves. Combine the
garlic, yoghourt, mint and parsley and add the cucumber.
Season to taste with salt and paprika.

Serves 4–6

Dressings & Sauces

A dressing on a salad can give scope for creative artistry, but one shouldn't lose sight of the fact that its prime purpose is to coat the lettuce leaves or pieces of sliced and chopped vegetables with a film of oil to prevent oxidation and the consequent loss of food value, crispness and flavour.

A badly flavoured or a badly seasoned dressing can spoil what would otherwise have been a good salad, so it needs to be prepared with thought and care. It is essential to follow a basic recipe for correct consistency, but of course personal preferences must come into play. Try experimenting with fresh herbs and spices when making both mayonnaise and French dressing. Remember that there are many other dressings as well as these two classics which can be used. Try to match the dressing to the salad – a 'heavy' salad is often better with a 'light' dressing, in other words rice with piquant dressing rather than mayonnaise is more appetizing.

The purpose of sauces is to moisten food and to add interest and flavour, and this of course applies equally to vegetarian wholefood cooking. Basic white sauce can be made with the 100% wholemeal flour, which gives the sauce a slightly 'off white' colour and unusual flavour. When it comes to a savoury brown sauce, or the vegetarian alternative to a meat-based gravy, the basic flavour comes from vegetables, yeast extracts, or soya sauce and seaweed. Like salad dressings, sauces are added to a meal to improve the overall quality and appearance, so care in preparation is essential – a poor sauce is almost worse than no sauce!

French dressing

Lemons, juice of 2
Cider or wine vinegar 4 tbsp (60 ml)
Salt 1½ tsp (7.5 ml)
Pepper ½ tsp (2.5 ml)
French mustard 1 tbsp (15 ml)
Raw brown sugar (optional) 2 tsp (10 ml)
Oil ¾ pt (450 ml)

Method 1
Put lemon juice, vinegar, salt, pepper, mustard and sugar into a jug. Whisk with a fork until evenly blended, then slowly work in the oil.

Method 2
Put all the ingredients together in a liquidizer goblet and blend for a few seconds.

Method 3
Shake all the ingredients together in a screw-topped jar. Store in the refrigerator.

Makes about 1 pt (600 ml)

Mayonnaise

Free-range egg 1
Salt ½ tsp (2.5 ml)
French mustard ½ tsp (2.5 ml)
Cider or wine vinegar 2 tsp (10 ml)
Oil ½ pt (300 ml)

Break the egg into a liquidizer goblet. Add the salt, mustard and vinegar. Blend for 10 seconds. While the liquidizer is switched on, slowly feed in the oil through the lid. As the oil is added, the mayonnaise will become thick.

To make the mayonnaise by hand, beat the egg, salt, mustard and vinegar together in a basin using a wooden spoon or balloon whisk, add the oil, *drop by drop*, until half the oil has been used. Continue adding in very small quantities until all the oil has been incorporated.

Makes ½ pt (300 ml)

Soured cream dressing

A tangy cream dressing particularly good with root vegetables

Fresh soured cream ¼ pt (142 ml)
Garlic clove, crushed 1
Cider or wine vinegar 1 tbsp (15 ml)

French mustard 1 tsp (5 ml)
Salt & pepper to taste

Combine the ingredients together. Adjust seasoning to taste with salt and pepper.

Makes about ¼ pt (150 ml)

Piquant dressing

A welcome change from French dressing

Oil ⅓ pt (200 ml)
Vinegar ⅓ pt (200 ml)
Water 4 fl.oz (100 ml)
Spring onions or chives, chopped 2 tbsp (30 ml)
Raw brown sugar 2 tsp (10 ml)
Paprika 1 tsp (5 ml)
Soya sauce 2 tsp (10 ml)
Salt ½ tsp (2.5 ml)
French mustard ½ tsp (2.5 ml)
Pepper to taste

Shake all the ingredients together in a screw-topped jar. Refrigerate and use as required.

Makes about 1 pt (600 ml)

Creamy paprika dressing

Raw brown sugar 1 tsp (5 ml)
Paprika 2 tsp (10 ml)
Salt 1 tsp (5 ml)
Cider or wine vinegar 4 tbsp (60 ml)
Free-range egg 1
Oil ⅓ pt (200 ml)

Combine the sugar and seasonings. Add the vinegar and egg. Beat well. Add the oil 1 tsp (5 ml) at a time until about one-quarter has been used. Slowly add remaining oil, beating well between each addition.

Alternatively, use the liquidizer method as for MAYONNAISE (*see page 103*).

Makes about ½ pt (300 ml)

Yoghourt dressing

A sharp and tangy dressing – not just for the weight conscious!

Natural yoghourt ¼ pt (142 ml)
Raw brown sugar or honey ½ tsp (2.5 ml)
Lemon, grated rind & juice of ½
Onion or spring onion, finely chopped 1 tbsp (15 ml)
Salt & pepper to taste

Combine all the ingredients together in a jug or basin until evenly mixed. Season to taste.

Makes about ¼ pt (150 ml)

Honey & lemon dressing

An ideal dressing for the weight conscious. It combines well with the fruit-based salads

Lemon, juice of 1
Clear honey 2 tbsp (30 ml)
Salt & pepper to taste

Whisk the ingredients together with a fork.

Makes about 4 tbsp (60 ml)

Nut cream

Use as an alternative to fresh dairy cream on breakfast cereal, stewed or fresh fruit

Whole blanched almonds or cashews 4 oz (100 g)
Warm water ¼–½ pt (150–300 ml)
Honey to taste
Lemon rind (optional)

Grind the nuts in a coffee mill, then transfer them to a basin. Gradually beat in the water to give a smooth, creamy paste. (Add sufficient water to give the required consistency.) Sweeten with honey to taste. Add a little grated lemon rind if wished.

Makes about ½ pt (300 ml)

Basic 'white' sauce

Wholemeal flour produces an oatmeal coloured sauce, rich in flavour and far removed from the bleached look of refined flour sauces. Variations in colour and texture can be produced by using alternatives, such as barley or maize flours

Butter or margarine 2 oz (50 g)
100% wholemeal flour 2 oz (50 g)
Milk 1 pt (568 ml)
Salt & pepper to taste

Melt the butter in a saucepan. Off the heat, stir in the flour, then cook for 1–2 minutes, stirring continuously. Slowly stir in the milk, until it is evenly blended. Bring to the boil, reduce heat and simmer for 2–3 minutes. Adjust seasoning to taste.

VARIATIONS
Cheese Add ½ tsp (2.5 ml) mustard powder with the flour. Stir in 4 oz (100 g) grated Cheddar cheese at the end of cooking. Do not boil after adding cheese.

Parsley Add 6 tbsp (90 ml) chopped parsley after the milk.

Makes 1 pt (600 ml)

Tomato sauce

An essential sauce in vegetarian cooking. Make this regularly and store in the refrigerator ready for use

Medium-sized onion 1
Tomatoes 12 oz (350 g)
Butter or margarine 1 oz (25 g)

Vegetable stock or water ½ pt (300 ml)
Garlic clove, crushed 1
Tomato paste 1 tbsp (15 ml)
Basil ½ tsp (2.5 ml)
Salt & pepper to taste

Chop the onion and tomatoes. Melt the butter in a large saucepan and fry the onion gently until transparent. Add the remaining ingredients, bring to the boil, then reduce heat and simmer uncovered for 20 minutes. Serve with pasta, rice dishes and savoury pies.

Makes 1 pt (600 ml)

Curry sauce

Medium-sized onion 1
Medium-sized carrots 2
Medium-sized cooking apples 2
Butter or margarine 2 oz (50 g)
Curry powder 1 tbsp (15 ml)
100% wholemeal flour 3 tbsp (45 ml)
Sultanas, soaked for 1 hour 2 oz (50 g)
Milk ½ pt (284 ml)
Vegetable stock ½ pt (300 ml)

Finely chop the onion, carrot and apple. Melt the butter and fry the prepared vegetables and apple until the onion is transparent. Stir in the curry powder and flour and cook for 2 minutes, stirring. Add the remaining ingredients, bring to the boil, reduce heat, cover and simmer for ½ hour.

Serve with hard-boiled eggs or diced cooked vegetables on a bed of boiled rice.

Makes about 1½ pt (900 ml)

Savoury brown sauce

Butter or margarine 2 oz (50 g)
Large onion 1
100% wholemeal flour 2 oz (50 g)

Vegetable stock 1 pt (600 ml)
Yeast extract 1 tbsp (15 ml)
Pepper to taste

Melt the butter. Skin and finely chop the onion and fry until golden brown. Stir in the flour and cook for 2 minutes, stirring occasionally. Pour in the stock and yeast extract, stirring. Bring to the boil, reduce heat, cover and simmer for 10 minutes. Adjust seasoning to taste. Serve with baked savoury dishes and nut rissoles.

If wished, strain the sauce, or blend in a liquidizer goblet, before serving.

Makes 1 pt (600 ml)

Savouries

According to the dictionary, the word 'savoury' means 'appetizing, salty or spiced, having relish'. In a meat meal when there is a savoury it is a small dish, meeting this definition, served at the beginning or end of the meal. What a vegetarian does is to elevate the importance of the savoury to the central position of the meal to replace the meat or fish.

Most hotels or restaurants faced with a vegetarian will be hard put to offer them anything more for a main dish than an omelette, and how boring this can become! Finding an alternative to the provision of meat, poulty or fish, which are so simple to provide, certainly does call for more imagination and more work, but the results can be creatively very rewarding, and the flavoursome dishes come as a great surprise when first experienced by meat eaters.

Cranks must have opened quite a few eyes to the extraordinary wealth of possible flavours and dishes that can be produced using only nuts and pulses, eggs and cheeses, rice, vegetables and cereals.

In recent years textured soya protein (TSP) has come on to the market with a meat-like texture and in a variety of meat-like forms. These are often sold with chemical colouring and flavouring aimed at getting as close as possible to the different meats and are therefore, with good reason, shunned by vegetarians or those concerned about the dangers of food additives. But the plain variety, carefully flavoured, can be very pleasant to eat and has its place as an alternative food, and it certainly helps those starting on a vegetarian diet to make the transition more easily. For this reason we have included some recipes using it.

We believe that vegetarian savoury dishes should be thought of as meals in their own right, containing the important food values. There is endless scope for experimenting with the making of savouries from a wholefood vegetarian larder, and we hope that our recipes will form just a starting-point for your voyage of discovery!

Brown rice risotto

Medium-sized onion 1
Medium-sized green pepper 1
Butter or margarine 1 oz (25 g)
Oil 3 tbsp (45 ml)
Broken cashew nuts 2 oz (50 g)
Medium-sized tomatoes 4
Long-grain brown rice, cooked 8 oz (225 g)
Garlic clove, crushed 1
Salt & pepper to taste

Chop the onion and slice the pepper. Heat the butter and oil in
a large saucepan. Add the green pepper, onion and cashews
and sauté until the vegetables are just tender, stirring occasionally. Chop the tomatoes and add to the pan with the rice
and garlic. Continue stirring over a gentle heat until the rice is
heated through. Adjust seasoning to taste.

Serves 4

Mushroom & potato pie

*A delicious mixture of mushrooms in sauce topped with creamed
potatoes – a Cranks favourite*

Potatoes 2 lb (900 g)
Celery sticks 4
Medium-sized onion 1
Mushrooms 1 lb (450 g)
Butter or margarine 3 oz (75 g)
Milk 4 tbsp (60 ml)
Garlic clove, crushed 2
Arrowroot 1½ tbsp (22.5 ml)
Milk ⅓ pt (200 ml)
Chopped parsley 2 tbsp (30 ml)
Dried thyme 1 tsp (5 ml)
Lemon juice 2 tsp (10 ml)
Salt & pepper to taste

Cook the potatoes in boiling water until tender. Grate the
celery, chop the onion and mushrooms. Drain the potatoes,

add 1 oz (25 g) butter and 4 tbsp (60 ml) milk, then mash until creamy. Season well. Melt the remaining butter in a large saucepan. Add the celery and onion and cook gently until the onion is transparent. Add the mushrooms and garlic, and cook, stirring occasionally, for 5 minutes. Blend the arrowroot with a little milk, stir in the remaining milk and stir into the mushrooms. Add the parsley, thyme and lemon juice, and season to taste. Simmer gently for 5 minutes. Turn the mixture into an ovenproof serving dish. Top with the mashed potato and place under a hot grill until heated through and golden, or place in the oven at 190°C (375°F/Mark 5) for about 20 minutes.

Serves 4–6

Vegetable fricassée

This versatile recipe can be served on a bed of freshly boiled rice or in individual ovenproof dishes topped with grated cheese and breadcrumbs and bubbled under the grill. Alternatively, use as a pie filling

Swede 12 oz (350 g)
Potatoes 8 oz (225 g)
Carrots 8 oz (225 g)
Large leek 1
Small cauliflower ½
Vegetable stock or water ¾ pt (450 ml)
Butter or margarine 2 oz (50 g)
100% wholemeal flour 2 oz (50 g)
Milk
Chopped parsley 6 tbsp (90 ml)
Lemon juice 1 tsp (5 ml)
Salt & pepper to taste

Cut the vegetables into ¾" (2 cm) chunks. Break the cauliflower into large florets. Bring the stock to the boil in a large saucepan, add the swede and carrots, return to the boil, then add the potatoes and simmer for 5 minutes. Add the leeks and cauliflower and cook for a further 3–5 minutes, until just tender but still crisp. Drain, reserving the stock. Keep the vegetables warm. Melt the butter in the saucepan, stir in the flour and cook for 1 minute. Make the stock up to ¾ pt (450 ml) with the milk. Add the stock and milk, stirring, and bring to the boil. Reduce the heat, add remaining ingredients and simmer for 2–3 minutes. Pour sauce over the vegetables and serve at once.

Serves 4–6

Macaroni in tomato sauce

This recipe also works with any other small pasta shapes

Wholemeal macaroni 6 oz (175 g)
Medium-sized red or green pepper 1
Courgettes 8 oz (225 g)
Butter or margarine 1 oz (25 g)
Tomato sauce (*see page 106*) 1 quantity

Cook the macaroni in boiling salted water for about 15 minutes, until just tender. Drain. Chop the pepper and slice the courgettes. Melt the butter in a saucepan, add the peppers and courgettes and sauté for about 3 minutes until tender but still crisp. Bring the tomato sauce to the boil, add the macaroni and vegetables, and heat to serving temperature.

Serves 4

Cranks nut roast

For a main course this is the ideal dish to present to anyone who is doubtful about the question of whether vegetarian food is satisfying, or exciting, or nutritious enough!

The actual preparation is easy, and the time taken not excessive, and there are, of course, many variations which can be attempted at a later date once the basic dish has been mastered

Basic recipe
Medium-sized onion 1
Butter or margarine 1 oz (25 g)
Mixed nuts, i.e. peanuts, walnuts, cashews etc. 8 oz (225 g)

Wholemeal bread 4 oz (100 g)
Vegetable stock or water ½ pt (300 ml)
Yeast extract 2 tsp (10 ml)
Mixed herbs 1 tsp (5 ml)
Salt & pepper to taste

Chop the onions and sauté in the butter until transparent. Grind the nuts and bread together in a liquidizer goblet, or coffee grinder, until quite fine. Heat the stock and yeast extract to boiling point, then combine all the ingredients together and mix well – the mixture should be fairly slack. Turn into a greased shallow baking dish, level the surface, sprinkle with a few breadcrumbs, and bake in the oven at 180°C (350°F/Mark 4) for 30 minutes, until golden brown. Garnish with fried onion rings, if wished.

Serves 4–6

VARIATIONS
Nut loaf with cheese and tomato layer Follow the basic recipe for NUT ROAST, but add only 3–4 tbsp (45–60 ml) of stock to give a firm mixture. Press half the mixture into a greased 1 lb (450 g) loaf tin. Cover with 2 sliced tomatoes and 2 oz (50 g) grated cheese and top with the remaining mixture. Bake as for NUT ROAST. Leave to cool in the tin, then remove carefully. Wrap in cling-wrap or greaseproof paper and put in the refrigerator. Cut into slices.

Rissoles Make up as for NUT LOAF but shape the mixture into 6 round 'cakes', coat with wholemeal breadcrumbs and fry in shallow oil for 3–5 minutes each side until golden brown. Serve hot or cold.

Cottage pie This is the Cranks vegetarian variation of Shepherd's Pie. Make up as for NUT ROAST, but add sufficient stock to give a loose texture, spoon into an ovenproof dish and top with 1½ lb (675 g) potatoes which have been boiled and mashed with a little milk and butter, pepper and salt. Bake in the oven at 200°C (400°F/Mark 6) for 20–30 minutes, until the potato is crisp and golden.

Jacket eggs Follow the recipe for NUT LOAF. Shell 4 hard-boiled free-range eggs and leave until cold. Encase the eggs in the NUT LOAF mixture. Roll in fresh wholemeal breadcrumbs and deep fry until golden. Drain and serve hot or cold.

Savoury carrot layer

A savoury pudding with two contrasting layers – a base of flavoursome carrot purée topped with a cheese custard

For the base
Carrots 1 lb (450 g)
Vegetable stock or water ¼–½ pt (150–300 ml)
Butter or margarine 1 oz (25 g)
Chopped parsley 2 tbsp (30 ml)
Soya sauce 1 tsp (5 ml)
Salt & pepper to taste

For the topping
Butter or margarine 1 oz (25 g)
100% wholemeal flour 1 oz (25 g)
Milk ¼ pt (142 ml)
Free-range eggs, beaten 3
Cheddar cheese, grated 3 oz (75 g)

Grate the carrots and put them in a saucepan with ¼ pt (150 ml) vegetable stock and the butter. Cover and simmer for about 15 minutes until the carrots are really tender. Add the parsley and soya sauce and blend the mixture in a liquidizer goblet until fairly smooth, adding a little more stock if necessary. Season to taste. Spread the mixture in the base of a greased ovenproof dish.

Melt the butter in a saucepan, stir in the flour and cook for 1 minute. Stir in the milk and continue simmering for a further 2 minutes. Off the heat, beat in the eggs and then the cheese. Adjust seasoning to taste. Pour over the carrot mixture then bake in the oven at 180°C (350°F/Mark 4) for about 45 minutes until just set. Serve at once.

Serves 4

Tomato & cheese pizza

Bread dough (*see page 214*) 1 lb (450 g)
Large onion 1
Oil 2 tbsp (30 ml)
Tomatoes 1 lb (450 g)
Garlic clove, crushed 1
Tomato paste 2 tbsp (30 ml)
Basil ½ tsp (2.5 ml)
Oregano ½ tsp (2.5 ml)
Salt & pepper to taste
Button mushrooms 4
Green pepper ½
Black olives 12
Cheddar cheese, grated 2 oz (50 g)

Knead the dough lightly, then roll out to a 12″ (30 cm) round or four 6″ (15 cm) rounds on a lightly floured surface. Place the dough on a greased baking sheet, cover with pieces of greased polythene and leave in a warm place for ½ hour to prove. Chop the onion, heat the oil in a saucepan and fry the onion until transparent. Reserve 2 tomatoes, chop the rest and add to the pan with the garlic, tomato paste, herbs and seasoning. Simmer gently, stirring occasionally until the mixture is 'pulpy'. Wash the mushrooms and cut each into 4 slices. Wash and trim the pepper and cut into 12 chunks. Spread the tomato mixture over the dough base. Decorate with the olives, mushroom slices, pepper and remaining tomatoes, cut into wedges, and sprinkle with cheese. Bake in the oven at 220°C (425°F/Mark 7) for about 25 minutes. Small pizzas will take about 15 minutes.

Serves 4

Macaroni cheese with vegetables

A variation on the classic recipe – other vegetables may be substituted as wished

Carrots 8 oz (225 g)
Courgettes 8 oz (225 g)

Celery sticks 4
Wholemeal cut macaroni 6 oz (175 g)
Vegetable stock or water ½ pt (300 ml)
Butter or margarine 2 oz (50 g)
100% wholemeal flour 2 oz (50 g)
Milk
Cheddar cheese 4 oz (100 g)
Salt & pepper to taste

Finely slice the vegetables. Cook the macaroni in boiling salted water for about 15 minutes until just tender. Drain in a colander or strainer. Put the prepared vegetables and the stock in a saucepan. Bring to the boil, then simmer for 5 minutes and drain, reserving the stock. Make the stock up to 1 pt (600 ml) with milk. Melt the butter in a saucepan, stir in the flour and cook for 1 minute. Stir in the stock and cook for a further few minutes. Off the heat, stir in 3 oz (75 g) cheese and season to taste. Add the macaroni and vegetables to the sauce. Spoon into a flame-proof serving dish, sprinkle with remaining cheese and place under a hot grill until golden.

Serves 4

Mushroom 'burgers'

Medium-sized onion 1
Mushrooms 8 oz (225 g)
Oil 2 tbsp (30 ml)
100% wholemeal flour 2 oz (50 g)
Water ¼ pt (150 ml)
Yeast extract 1 tsp (5 ml)
Lemon juice 1 tsp (5 ml)
Ground nutmeg to taste
Fresh wholemeal breadcrumbs 3 oz (75 g)
Free-range egg, hardboiled, shelled & finely chopped 1
Salt & pepper to taste

To coat
Free-range eggs, beaten 2
100% wholemeal breadcrumbs 4 oz (100 g)
Oil for frying

Chop the onion and mushrooms. Heat the oil in a saucepan and sauté the onion until transparent. Add the mushrooms and cook 1–2 minutes, stirring. Stir in the flour, then the water, yeast extract, lemon juice and nutmeg. Simmer gently for 5 minutes, stirring frequently. Off the heat, stir in the breadcrumbs and chopped egg, then adjust seasoning to taste. Leave until cold. With floured hands shape the mixture into 8 'cakes', dip in the beaten egg and then in the breadcrumbs. Fry in shallow oil over a medium heat for about 5 minutes until each side is golden brown. Drain on absorbent kitchen paper. Serve hot or cold.

Makes 8 'burgers'

'Moussaka'

This is a vegetarian version of the traditional Greek moussaka using TSP (Textured Soya Protein) instead of minced meat

Medium-sized onion 1
Oil 6 tbsp (90 ml)
Garlic clove 1
Mushrooms 2 oz (50 g)
Tomatoes 2
Tomato paste 1 tbsp (15 ml)
Water ¼ pt (150 ml)
Yeast extract 1 tsp (5 ml)
TSP minced style 2½ oz (60 g)
Vegetable stock cube 1
Parsley, chopped 1 tbsp (15 ml)
Large aubergine 1
100% wholemeal flour 2 tbsp (30 ml)
Cheddar cheese, grated 2 oz (50 g)
Free-range eggs 3
Natural yoghourt ¼ pt (142 ml)

Chop onion, mushrooms and tomatoes and thinly slice the aubergine. Heat 2 tbsp (30 ml) oil in a saucepan, sauté onion until transparent. Add crushed garlic, mushrooms, tomatoes, tomato paste, water, yeast extract, TSP, stock cube and parsley. Stir well, bring to the boil, reduce heat and simmer, covered, for 10 minutes. Dust the aubergine slices in the flour, then fry in remaining oil until soft. In an ovenproof dish layer up the aubergines and TSP mixture finishing with a layer of aubergines. Sprinkle with cheese. Whisk together the eggs and yoghourt and pour over the pie. Bake in the oven at 180°C (350°F/Mark 4) for 35–40 minutes until golden brown.

Serves 4

Spicy chick peas

Chick peas are very much underrated, although they can give a good protein base as well as an unusual flavour and texture to savoury dishes

Chick peas, soaked overnight 8 oz (225 g)
Butter or margarine 1 oz (25 g)
Medium-sized onion 1
Tomatoes 1 lb (450 g)
Spinach 8 oz (225 g)
Ground cumin 1 tsp (5 ml)
Oregano 1 tsp (5 ml)
Paprika 1 tsp (5 ml)
Cheddar cheese, grated 4 oz (100 g)
Salt to taste
Natural yoghourt to garnish
Paprika to garnish

Place pre-soaked chick peas in a saucepan, just cover with water and simmer for about 45 minutes until tender. Drain, reserving ⅓ pt (200 ml) cooking liquor. Weigh out 4 oz (100 g) chick peas and blend in a liquidizer goblet with the cooking liquor until smooth. Chop the onion and tomatoes, and shred the spinach. Melt the butter in a saucepan and sauté the onion until transparent. Add cumin, and whole chick peas, and cook, stirring for 2 minutes. Stir in the spinach, tomatoes and blended chick peas, herbs and seasonings. Bring to the boil, reduce heat and simmer for 5 minutes. Off the heat, stir in the cheese until melted. Adjust seasoning to taste.

Serve at once, topped with yoghourt and sprinkled with a little paprika.

Serves 4–6

Eggs Florentine

Spinach 1 lb (450 g)
Butter or margarine 2 oz (50 g)
Salt & pepper to taste
Ground nutmeg to taste
Small onion 1
100% wholemeal flour 1 oz (25 g)
Mustard powder 1 tsp (5 ml)
Milk ½ pt (284 ml)
Cheddar cheese, grated 4 oz (100 g)
Free-range eggs, hardboiled & shelled 4
Brown rice, freshly cooked 4 oz (100 g)
Toasted breadcrumbs 1 tbsp (15 ml)

Shred the spinach. Melt half the butter in a saucepan, add the spinach and cook over medium heat for a few minutes, stirring frequently, until just tender. Season with salt, pepper and nutmeg. Keep warm. Chop the onion. Melt the remaining butter in a saucepan and sauté the onion until transparent. Stir in the flour and mustard and cook for 1 minute. Add the milk, stirring, bring to the boil and simmer for a few minutes. Off the heat, stir in the cheese. Arrange the rice in a warmed serving dish, spoon the spinach in the centre. Arrange halved eggs on top and pour over the eggs. Sprinkle the breadcrumbs over and serve at once.

Serves 4

Aubergine Parmesan

A hearty and warming savoury with an Italian flavour

Potatoes 1 lb (450 g)
Aubergines 1 lb (450 g)
Oil ¼ pt (150 ml)

Butter or margarine 2 oz (50 g)
Medium-sized onion 1
Tomatoes 4
100% wholemeal flour 2 tbsp (30 ml)
Milk ¼ pt (142 ml)
Garlic clove, crushed 1
Basil ½ tsp (2.5 ml)
Oregano ½ tsp (2.5 ml)
Salt & pepper to taste
Parmesan cheese 3 tbsp (45 ml)
Wholemeal breadcrumbs 3 tbsp (45 ml)
Chopped parsley to garnish

Cut the potatoes into large dice and cook in boiling water for about 10 minutes, until just tender. Drain, reserving ½ pt (300 ml) cooking liquor. Dice the aubergines and chop the onion and tomatoes. Heat the oil and sauté the aubergines until golden and tender. Melt half the butter and sauté the onion until transparent. Add the tomatoes, stir in the flour and cook for 1 minute. Add the potato liquor, milk, garlic, herbs and seasoning. Bring to the boil, reduce heat and simmer for 15–20 minutes. Spoon the potatoes and aubergines into a warmed serving dish. Spoon over the tomato sauce. Mix together the breadcrumbs and Parmesan cheese and sprinkle over the sauce. Dot with the remaining butter. Place in the oven at 200°C (400°F/Mark 6) for about 20 minutes until heated through. Sprinkle with chopped parsley.

Serves 4–6

Millet & vegetable gratinée

The contrasting flavours and textures of millet and vegetables provide a satisfying savoury dish

Millet 4 oz (100 g)
Water 1 pt (600 ml)
Butter or margarine 3 oz (75 g)
Medium-sized leeks 2
Large carrot 1

Celery sticks 4
100% wholemeal flour 1 oz (25 g)
Milk 1 pt (568 ml)
Chopped parsley 3 tbsp (45 ml)
Sage 1 tsp (5 ml)
Lemon, grated rind & juice of ½
Salt & pepper to taste
Cheddar cheese, grated 4 oz (100 g)

Cook the millet in the measured boiling water until just tender and all the water has been absorbed. Slice the leeks, grate the carrot and finely slice the celery. Melt 2 oz (50 g) butter in a saucepan, add the vegetables and sauté for 10–15 minutes, stirring frequently. Add the millet and stir over very gentle heat to keep warm. Meanwhile, melt the remaining butter in a saucepan. Stir in the flour and cook for 1 minute. Stir in the milk, herbs, lemon rind and juice, and bring to the boil. Reduce heat and simmer for 2 minutes. Pour it over the vegetables and stir well. Adjust seasoning with salt and pepper. Transfer to a warmed serving dish, sprinkle with cheese, and 'bubble' under a hot grill until golden brown.

Serves 4–6

Lentil & buckwheat slice

Delicious served hot with green vegetables or cold as part of a packed lunch

Buckwheat 4 oz (100 g)
Medium-sized onion 1
Medium-sized carrot 1
Oil 2 tbsp (30 ml)
Red lentils 6 oz (175 g)
Vegetable stock or water 1½ pt (900 ml)
Chopped parsley 2 tbsp (30 ml)
Rosemary, powdered ½ tsp (2.5 ml)
Yeast extract 1 tsp (5 ml)
Salt & pepper to taste
Nutmeg to taste

Toast the buckwheat until golden brown. Chop the onion and carrot. Heat the oil in a saucepan and sauté the onion and carrot until the onion is transparent. Add the buckwheat and lentils, and the remaining ingredients. Bring to the boil, reduce heat and simmer for about ½ hour, until all the liquid is absorbed. Press the mixture into a greased 10″ (25 cm) flan tin, and bake in the oven at 200°C (400°F/Mark 6) for ½ hour. Serve hot, or cold in wedges with chutney.

Serves 6

Golden vegetable layer

Swede 1 lb (450 g)
Large potato 1
Large carrot 1
Butter or margarine 2 oz (50 g)
Salt & pepper to taste
Tomato sauce (*see page 106*) 1 quantity
Chopped parsley to garnish

Chop the swede, potato and carrot and steam for 20–25 minutes until just tender. Boil the tomato sauce until it becomes a thick purée. Keep warm. Roughly mash the vegetables (do not let them become smooth) with the butter and season generously with salt and pepper. Spoon the mixture into a warmed serving dish, top with the tomato sauce and sprinkle with chopped parsley. Serve at once.

This dish could be prepared in advance and heated through in a medium-hot oven for about ½ hour.

Serves 4

Oriental beanshoots

An exotic blend of ingredients gives the beanshoots an exciting sweet and sour flavour

Medium-sized onion 1
Medium-sized carrot 1
Large green pepper ½

Celery sticks 2
Butter or margarine 1 oz (25 g)
Cucumber ¼
Tomatoes 8 oz (225 g)
Garlic clove, crushed 1
Pineapple juice ½ pt (300 ml)
Arrowroot 1 tbsp (15 ml)
Cider vinegar 3 tbsp (45 ml)
Raw brown sugar 2 tbsp (30 ml)
Vegetable stock cube 1
Soya sauce 2 tsp (10 ml)
Ground ginger ½ tsp (2.5 ml)
Ground bay leaf, pinch
Salt & pepper to taste
Beanshoots 12 oz (350 g)

Chop the onion, finely dice the carrot and green pepper, thinly slice the celery. Melt the butter in a large saucepan and add the onion, carrot, pepper and celery, and sauté until the onion is transparent. Chop the cucumber and tomatoes and add all the remaining ingredients except the beanshoots. Bring to the boil, reduce the heat, cover and simmer until the vegetables are just tender. Stir in the beanshoots and cook for a further 2 minutes. Serve at once.

Serves 4

Mushroom Stroganoff

Large onion 1
Celery sticks 4
Mushrooms 12 oz (350 g)
Butter or margarine 2 oz (50 g)
100% wholemeal flour 1 tbsp (15 ml)
Water ¼ pt (150 ml)
Yeast extract 1 tsp (5 ml)
Thyme ½ tsp (2.5 ml)
Ground bay leaf, pinch
Soured cream ¼ pt (142 ml)

Salt & pepper to taste
Chopped parsley to garnish

Slice the onion, celery and mushrooms. Melt half the butter in a saucepan, and sauté onion and celery until the onion is transparent. Add remaining butter and allow to melt, add mushrooms and stir occasionally over medium heat for 2–3 minutes. Stir in the flour, then add the water, yeast extract and herbs. Bring to the boil, reduce heat and simmer, uncovered, for 2–3 minutes. Off the heat, stir in the soured cream and adjust seasoning to taste. Heat very gently to serving temperature. Serve at once on a bed of freshly cooked rice. Sprinkle with parsley.

Serves 4

Vegetarian goulash

Medium-sized onion 1
Medium-sized courgettes 2
Medium-sized carrots 2
Small white cabbage ½
Oil 3 tbsp (45 ml)
Paprika 1 tbsp (15 ml)
Caraway seeds ½ tsp (2.5 ml)
Mixed herbs ½ tsp (2.5 ml)
Nutmeg, pinch
Tomato juice 1 pt (600 ml)
Water ½ pt (300 ml)
Vegetable stock cube 1
Salt to taste
Soured cream or natural yoghourt ¼ pt (142 ml)

Slice the onion and courgettes, dice the carrots and finely shred the cabbage. Heat the oil in a large saucepan and sauté the onion and carrot until the onion is transparent. Add the courgettes and cabbage and cook over medium heat for 10 minutes, stirring frequently. Stir in the paprika, caraway seeds, herbs and nutmeg, then add the tomato juice, water, and stock cube. Cover and simmer for about 20 minutes until

the vegetables are just tender. Adjust seasoning with salt.
Spoon the goulash into a warmed serving dish and drizzle with
soured cream or yoghourt. Serve at once.

Serves 4–6

Express cheese pudding

Takes only minutes to prepare!

Small onion 1
Wholemeal breadcrumbs 4 oz (125 g)
Cheddar cheese, grated 4 oz (125 g)
Free-range eggs 2
French mustard 1 tsp (5 ml)
Milk ¾ pt (426 ml)
Salt & pepper ¼ tsp (1.25 ml) of each
Chopped parsley to garnish

Peel and roughly chop the onion. Put all the ingredients
together in a liquidizer goblet and blend until smooth. Pour
the mixture into a greased shallow baking dish and bake in the
oven at 200°C (400°F/Mark 6) for about 45 minutes, until set
and golden brown. Sprinkle with chopped parsley.

Serves 4

Curried split peas

Green split peas, soaked overnight 8 oz (225 g)
Medium-sized onion 1
Medium-sized carrots 2
Butter or margarine 2 oz (50 g)
Medium-sized cooking apples 2
Curry powder 1 tbsp (15 ml)
100% wholemeal flour 3 tbsp (45 ml)
Sultanas, soaked for 1 hour 2 oz (50 g)
Milk ½ pt (284 ml)
Salt & pepper to taste
Toasted coconut to garnish

Cover the peas with fresh water and bring to the boil. Simmer, covered, for about ½ hour. Take off the heat and keep to one side. Finely chop the onion and dice the carrots. Melt the butter in a saucepan and sauté the prepared vegetables until the onion is transparent. Chop the apples. Stir the curry powder and flour into the sautéed vegetables. Drain the peas, reserving ½ pt (300 ml) of cooking liquor and add the split peas and liquor to the pan with the remaining ingredients, except the toasted coconut. Bring to the boil, reduce heat and simmer for about ½ hour. Adjust seasoning to taste. Serve on a bed of freshly cooked rice and garnish with toasted coconut.

Serves 6

Haricot beans in tomato sauce

A bean stew with a difference

Haricot beans 4 oz (100 g)
Large courgette 1
Large green pepper 1
Medium-sized onion 1
Tomatoes 8 oz (225 g)
Butter or margarine 2 oz (50 g)
100% wholemeal flour 1 oz (25 g)
Milk ¾ pt (426 ml)
Bay leaf 1
Garlic clove, crushed 1
Basil ½ tsp (2.5 ml)
Salt & pepper to taste

Soak the beans overnight. Strain, cover with fresh water, bring to the boil, reduce heat and simmer for 2 hours, checking the water from time to time. Slice the courgette, cut the green pepper into strips, and chop the onion and tomatoes. Melt half the butter in a saucepan and sauté the courgettes and pepper until just tender. Remove from the pan. Add the remaining butter to the pan and sauté the onion until transparent. Stir in the flour, and then the milk. Bring to the boil, reduce heat. Add the tomatoes, bay leaf, garlic and basil, and simmer for 10 minutes. Stir in the drained beans, courgette and pepper. Adjust seasoning to taste. If wished, sprinkle with grated cheese before serving.

Serves 4–6

Winter hot pot

Medium-sized onion 1
Carrots 8 oz (225 g)
Medium-sized potato 1
Large parsnip 1
Turnips 4 oz (100 g)
Swede 8 oz (225 g)
Butter or margarine 2 oz (50 g)
Pot barley, soaked 2 oz (50 g)
Water 1½ pt (900 ml)
Yeast extract 1 tbsp (15 ml)
Garlic cloves, chopped 2
Bay leaf 1
Thyme ½ tsp (2.5 ml)
100% wholemeal flour 1 oz (25 g)
Water 2 tbsp (30 ml)
Salt & pepper to taste

Chop all the vegetables. Melt the butter in a large saucepan and sauté the onions and carrots until the onions are transparent. Add the remaining vegetables, pot barley, water, yeast extract, garlic, bay leaf and thyme. Bring to the boil, reduce heat, cover and simmer for 15–20 minutes until the vegetables are just tender. Blend flour and water and stir into hot pot – simmer for 2–3 minutes to thicken. Adjust seasoning to taste with salt & pepper.

Serves 4–6

'Macro' rice

Originally Cranks introduced this recipe to cater for the needs of those on a macrobiotic diet. Since then it has become one of the most popular daily dishes in the restaurants

PAUL WILLIAMS

Soups

1 Country vegetable soup
2 Carrot potage
3 Cream of spinach & courgette soup
4 Russian vegetable soup
5 Wholemeal rusks
6 Cheese scones

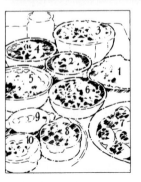

Salads

1. Chicory & oranges with cheese dressing
2. Waldorf salad
3. Green salad
4. Wholewheat mayonnaise
5. Hawaiian rice salad
6. Italian pasta salad
7. Eggs Indienne
8. Hummus
9. Cream cheese & cashew nut pâté
10. Mushroom pâté

PAUL WILLIAMS

Savouries

1 Jacket eggs
2 Nut loaf with cheese &
      tomato layer
3 Green salad
4 Aubergine & red bean stew
5 Nut roast
6 Tomato & cheese pizza
7 Leek & cheese flan
8 Homity pies
9 Spinach roulade

PAUL WILLIAMS

Puddings & Desserts

1 Lemon meringue pie
2 Sticky prune cake
3 Orange & banana trifle
4 Lemon cheesecake
5 Sunshine pie
6 Creamy bran & apple
  chunks

PAUL WILLIAMS

Cakes & Biscuits

1 Millet & peanut cookies
2 Fruit scones
3 Brown sugar meringues
4 Iced carrot cake
5 Carob chip cookies
6 Coconut biscuits
7 Truffle triangle
8 Date & coconut gateau
9 Drop scones
10 Barabrith
11 Honey buns
12 Honey cake

Breads

1. Barley bread
2. Cranks wholemeal loaf
3. Wholemeal rolls
4. Cheese loaf
5. Bran loaf
6. Oatmeal soda bread
7. Chelsea buns
8. Spiced currant bread
9. Pumpernickel
10. Rye bread

Cranks Cheese Baps

These won an *Evening Standard* award for the best sandwich in London!

Juices

1 Carrot, orange & honey drink
2 Raspberry yoghourt drink
3 Tiger's milk – a Gaylord Hauser recipe
4 Cranks homemade lemonade
5 Watercress, tomato & apple drink
6 Tomato juice
7 Curvacious cocktail – a Gaylord Hauser recipe
8 Cucumber, lemon & honey drink

Long-grain rice 8 oz (225 g)
Medium-sized onions 2
Oil 4 tbsp (60 ml)
Parsley, chopped 4 tbsp (60 ml)
Soya sauce 2 tbsp (30 ml)
Salt & pepper to taste

Cook the rice in boiling water for 30–40 minutes until just tender. (Half way through the cooking time, start cooking the onions.) Slice the onions. Heat the oil in a frying pan and sauté the onions until transparent, without browning them. Add the parsley and stir through for 1 minute. Drain the rice and add to the onions in the frying pan. Add the soya sauce and stir through. Adjust seasoning to taste. Serve at once – or if wished, allow to cool and serve as a salad course.

Serves 4

Savoury mix

There has always been a need within the vegetarian diet for a protein-based mixture to replace sausage meat and minced meats. Here is Cranks solution to that need! Use it to fill pies, pasties and savoury rolls

Yellow split peas 4 oz (100 g)
Medium-sized carrot 1
Medium-sized onion 1
Water ¾ pt (450 ml)
Coarse oatmeal 6 oz (175 g)
Oil 1 tbsp (15 ml)
Garlic cloves, crushed 2
Yeast extract 2 tsp (10 ml)
Tomato paste 1 tbsp (15 ml)
Thyme 1 tsp (5 ml)
Sage 1 tsp (5 ml)
Parsley, chopped 2 tbsp (30 ml)
Fresh breadcrumbs 4 oz (100 g)
Salt & pepper to taste

Soak the peas in water overnight. Grate the carrot and onion. Put the peas and water in a saucepan with the carrot and onion. Bring to the boil, reduce heat and simmer, covered, for 20 minutes. Add the oatmeal and cook for a further 10 minutes. Off the heat, stir in the remaining ingredients and leave to cool. Adjust seasoning to taste.

Makes about 2 lb (1 kg)

Lentil & cheese wedges

Red lentils 8 oz (225 g)
Water ¾ pt (450 ml)
Large onion 1
Butter or margarine 1 oz (25 g)
Cheddar cheese, grated 4 oz (100 g)
Mixed herbs 1 tsp (5 ml)
Free-range egg 1
Wholemeal breadcrumbs 1 oz (25 g)
Salt & pepper to taste

Cook the lentils in the measured water until soft and all the liquid has been absorbed. Chop the onion, then melt the butter in a saucepan and fry the onion until transparent. Combine all the ingredients together and press into an oiled 9″ (23 cm) sandwich tin. Bake in the oven at 190°C (375°F/Mark 5) for 30 minutes. Serve hot or cold, in wedges.

Serves 6

Surrey raised pie

Makes an impressive centrepiece on a buffet table

Hot water crust pastry (*see page 231*) 1 quantity
Savoury mix (*see page 129*) ¾ quantity
Tomatoes, sliced 4
Salad ingredients to garnish

Use three-quarters of the pastry to line a 6″ (15 cm) round, deep cake tin. Place half the savoury mix in the base of the tin.

Top with the sliced tomatoes and finish with a layer of savoury mix. Roll out the remaining pastry and use to top the pie. Seal the edges well and make a decorative edge. Make a hole in the centre of the pie. Use the trimmings to make 'leaves' and arrange on the top of the pie. Bake in the oven at 200°C (400°F/Mark 6) for about 45 minutes. If overbrowning, cover the pastry with foil. Allow to cool in the tin, remove carefully and serve on a large plate garnished with salad ingredients.

'Soya mix' — using Textured Soya Protein

Using TSP makes this a quickly prepared and easy alternative savoury filling

Medium-sized onion 1
Butter or margarine 1 oz (25 g)
Tomatoes 8 oz (225 g)
Pkt (natural) Protoveg flavour, minced style 5 oz (142 g)
Rice flour 1 oz (25 g)
Basil 1 tsp (5 ml)
Yeast extract 1 tsp (5 ml)
Water ¼ pt (150 ml)
Free-range egg, beaten 1
Salt & pepper to taste
Fresh wholemeal breadcrumbs 2 oz (50 g)

Chop the onion and tomatoes, then melt the butter in a saucepan and sauté the onion until transparent. Add the tomatoes and cook for a further few minutes until 'pulpy'. Stir in Protoveg, rice flour, basil, yeast extract and water and simmer gently for 5 minutes. Off the heat, stir in the beaten egg, season generously with salt and pepper, and stir in the breadcrumbs. Use as a pie filling. If wished, add extra stock to give a more moist consistency.

Soya, egg & vegetable pie

Carrots 4 oz (100 g)
Shelled fresh peas, or green beans 4 oz (100 g)
Gelozone jelling compound 1 tbsp (15 ml)

Vegetable stock 1 pt (600 ml)
Wholemeal shortcrust pastry, made with 14 oz (400 g) flour
  (*see page 230*)
Soya mix (*see page 131*) ½ quantity
Free-range eggs, hard boiled & shelled 3

Dice the carrots and steam with the peas or beans for 5 minutes. Cool. Mix the Gelozone with a little stock to give a smooth paste; add the remaining stock, then simmer for 2 minutes. Leave to cool. Meanwhile, roll out two-thirds of the pastry and use to line a 2 lb (900 g) loaf tin. Layer up the soya mix and vegetables, arranging the whole eggs along the length of the pie, in the centre. Pour in the cooked Gelozone until it reaches the top of the pie. Roll out the remaining pastry and use to top the pie. Seal the edges well. Make a large hole in the centre. Using the pastry trimmings to make leaves and arrange these around the 'steam hole' on top of the pie. Bake in the oven at 200°C (400°F/Mark 6) for about 40 minutes. Leave in the tin until completely cold. Remove carefully and slice.

Serves 6–8

Soya 'burgers' in salad baps

The wholefood answer to the fast food craze!

Soya mix (*see page 131*) ½ quantity
Oil 2 tbsp (30 ml)
Wholemeal baps 4 (*see page 241*)
Butter or margarine 4 oz (100 g)
Small lettuce 1
Large tomatoes 2
Mayonnaise (*see page 103*) 4 tbsp (60 ml)

Shape the soya mix into 4 'burgers'. Fry gently in a minimum of oil until golden on both sides. Split and butter the baps, shred the lettuce and slice the tomatoes. Arrange a little shredded lettuce on the base of each bap. Fill with a soya 'burger', sliced tomatoes and mayonnaise.

Makes 4

Buckwheat pancakes

Buckwheat flour is becoming increasingly popular as an alternative to wheat flour in pancake batters. The resulting pancakes are dark in colour and have the distinctive buckwheat flavour

Buckwheat flour 2 oz (50 g)
100% wholemeal flour 2 oz (50 g)
Salt, pinch
Free-range egg 1
Milk ½ pt (284 ml)
Oil or margarine for frying

Put the flours and salt into a basin. Make a 'well' in the centre, break the egg into the 'well', then whisk in the milk a little at a time, until the batter is the consistency of pouring cream. Thin with a little extra milk if necessary. Lightly oil a small frying pan, heat gently, then, holding the pan at an angle, pour in a little of the batter, swirling it round the pan to give a thin layer. Cook over medium heat until the batter is set. Turn with a palette knife and brown on the second side.

SERVING SUGGESTIONS
Sprinkle with cheese and roll up.
Spoon a little ratatouille in the centre and fold up.
Serve with soured cream and honey.

Makes 8–10 pancakes

Stir-fried leeks with mushrooms

Small leeks 8
Button mushrooms 1½ lb (675)
Butter or margarine 2 oz (50 g)
Raw brown sugar ½ tsp (2.5 ml)
Turmeric ½ tsp (2.5 ml)
Ground ginger 1 tsp (5 ml)
100% wholemeal flour 4 tbsp (60 ml)
Vegetable stock ⅓ pt (200 ml)

Slice the leeks and quarter the mushrooms. Melt the butter in a large frying pan. Add the leeks and mushrooms and stir constantly over a high heat until the vegetables are just tender. Combine the remaining ingredients, except the flour and stock. Sprinkle the flour over the vegetables, stir through, then add the flavoured stock. Bring to the boil, reduce heat and simmer for 5 minutes.

Serves 6

Cauliflower cheese

Medium-sized cauliflower 1
Cheese sauce (*see page 106*) 1 quantity
Fresh wholemeal breadcrumbs 4 tbsp (60 ml)
Grated cheese 4 oz (100 g)

Break the cauliflower into large florets. Steam for 10–12 minutes, depending on size, until just tender. Turn into an ovenproof serving dish, spoon over the sauce. Sprinkle with the breadcrumbs and cheese and 'bubble' under a hot grill or in a hot oven until golden.

Serves 4

Buckwheat bake

Truly original in flavour, this really should be tasted – season generously for best results

Medium-sized onion 1
Tomatoes 4
Oil 2 tbsp (30 ml)
Buckwheat 3 oz (75 g)
Long-grain rice 1 oz (25 g)
Water ½ pt (300 ml)
Basil 1 tsp (5 ml)
Salt & pepper to taste

Chop the onion and tomatoes. Heat the oil in a saucepan and fry the onions until transparent. Add the tomatoes and stir until softened. Stir in the buckwheat and rice and cook for 1 minute. Add the remaining ingredients. Bring to the boil, reduce heat, cover and simmer until the liquid has been absorbed (about 20 minutes). Adjust seasoning, then turn the mixture into a greased 7" (18 cm) square, shallow cake tin. Bake in the oven at 190°C (375°F/Mark 5) for 30 minutes. Serve hot or cold.

Serves 4–6

Savoury potato dish

Potatoes 2 lb (900 g)
Milk ½ pt (284 ml)
Free-range egg 1
Salt ½ tsp (2.5 ml)
Pepper ¼ tsp (1.25 ml)
Nutmeg ¼ tsp (1.25 ml)
Butter or margarine 1 oz (25 g)
Parsley, chopped to garnish

Grease a shallow ovenproof dish large enough to hold the potatoes in a single layer. Dice the unpeeled potatoes and spread them over the base of the dish. Beat the milk and egg together, add the seasoning and nutmeg, and pour over the potatoes. Dot with butter and bake, uncovered, for about 45 minutes at 200°C (400°F/Mark 6) until the potatoes are tender. Serve immediately, garnished with parsley.

Serves 4

Spiced chick pea croquettes

This generously spiced mixture makes delicious and colourful croquettes which may be served either hot or cold

Chick peas 8 oz (225 g)
Free-range egg 1
Parsley, chopped 3 tbsp (45 ml)
Garlic cloves, crushed 2
Ground cumin 1 tsp (5 ml)
Basil 1 tsp (5 ml)
Salt 1 tsp (5 ml)

Turmeric ½ tsp (2.5 ml)
Cayenne, pinch

Coating
Beaten egg
Bran

Soak chick peas overnight, then drain. Cook the chick peas in boiling water for 1 hour until fairly soft. Drain, reserving the cooking liquor. Grind or mash the peas and mix with 3 tbsp (45 ml) reserved cooking liquor and the remaining ingredients. Form the mixture into 8 croquettes. Dip in the beaten egg and then in bran and deep fry for a few minutes until golden brown. Drain on absorbent kitchen paper.

Makes 8 croquettes

'No-cook rissoles'

Mixed nuts 4 oz (100 g)
Cottage cheese 8 oz (225 g)
Parsley, chopped 3 tbsp (45 ml)
Onion, finely chopped 1 tbsp (15 ml)
Salt & pepper to taste
Sunnybisk or Weetabix breakfast cereal, crushed 3

Roughly grind the nuts. Combine the cottage cheese, nuts, parsley, onion and sufficient salt and pepper to taste. Shape the mixture into 4 'cakes'. Coat in crushed cereal and refrigerate until required.

Makes 4 rissoles

Stuffed cabbage leaves

The colour and texture of cabbage leaves give this dish an attractive appearance

Medium-sized green cabbage leaves 8
Long-grain brown rice 3 oz (75 g)
Medium-sized onion 1
Oil 2 tbsp (30 ml)

Sultanas 1 tbsp (15 ml)
Tomato juice ¼ pt (150 ml)
Mint, chopped 1 tsp (5 ml)
Salt 1 tsp (5 ml)
Flaked almonds 1 oz (25 g)
Vegetable stock cube 1
Water ¼ pt (150 ml)

Steam the cabbage leaves for about 5 minutes. Remove the coarse central stalk. Boil the rice in water for 20 minutes then drain. Chop the onion. Heat the oil in a saucepan and sauté the onion until transparent. Add the rice, sultanas and tomato juice and simmer until the tomato juice is absorbed. Stir in the mint, salt and almonds. Use the rice mixture to fill the cabbage leaves, roll into neat shapes. Place in an ovenproof casserole dish. Dissolve the stock cube in water and pour over the cabbage leaves. Cover and bake in the oven at 180°C (350°F/Mark 4) for about 30 minutes. Serve with baked tomatoes and roast potatoes.

Serves 4

Creamy leek croustade

The delightful contrast in flavours and textures of this layered savoury makes it ideal for a dinner party

Base
Fresh wholemeal breadcrumbs 6 oz (175 g)
Butter or margarine 2 oz (50 g)
Cheddar cheese, grated 4 oz (100 g)
Mixed nuts, chopped 4 oz (100 g)
Mixed herbs ½ tsp (2.5 ml)
Garlic clove, crushed 1

Sauce
Medium-sized leeks 3
Tomatoes 4
Butter or margarine 2 oz (50 g)
100% wholemeal flour 1 oz (25 g)
Milk ½ pt (284 ml)

Salt & pepper to taste
Fresh wholemeal breadcrumbs 4 tbsp (60 ml)

Put the breadcrumbs in a basin, rub in the butter, then add the remaining ingredients. Press the mixture into a 11 × 7" (28 × 18 cm) tin. Bake in the oven at 220°C (425°F/Mark 7) for 15–20 minutes, until golden brown.

Meanwhile, slice the leeks and chop the tomatoes. Melt the butter in a saucepan. Sauté the leeks for 5 minutes, then stir in the flour. Add the milk, stirring constantly, then bring to the boil, reduce heat to a simmer. Add the remaining ingredients, except breadcrumbs, and simmer for a few minutes to soften the tomatoes. Check seasoning. Spoon the vegetable mixture over the base, sprinkle with breadcrumbs and heat through in the oven at 180°C (350°F/Mark 4) for 20 minutes. Serve at once.

Serves 6

Spinach roulade

Don't be daunted by the preparation and time involved in this recipe. Perseverance is all that is needed to produce this impressive roulade

Medium-sized onion 1
Fresh spinach 8 oz (225 g)
Butter or margarine 1 oz (25 g)
Parsley, chopped 2 tbsp (30 ml)
Salt & pepper to taste
Ground nutmeg to taste
Free-range eggs 4
100% wholemeal flour 2 oz (50 g)
Cottage cheese 8 oz (225 g)
Fresh chives or spring onions, chopped 2–3 tbsp (30–45 ml)

Grease and line a swiss roll tin with greaseproof paper. Finely chop the onion and remove the coarse stems from the spinach. Melt the butter in a saucepan and sauté the onion until transparent. Add the spinach and cook over high heat, stirring frequently, until no moisture remains. Off the heat, stir in the parsley and season generously with salt, pepper and nutmeg. Turn the spinach mixture on to a clean working surface and chop. Leave to cool (*do not purée the spinach*). Whisk the eggs and a pinch of the salt in a basin until thick and creamy – i.e. until the trail of the whisk stays in the mixture. Fold in the cooled spinach and the flour carefully, then turn the mixture into the prepared tin. Level the surface and bake in the oven at 200°C (400°F/Mark 6) for 10–12 minutes, until even and firm to the touch. Turn out on to a piece of greaseproof paper and roll up like a swiss roll, starting from a short edge and keeping the paper in between the roll. Leave to cool on a wire tray. Mix the cottage cheese with the chives. Carefully unroll the 'roulade' and spread with cottage cheese. Re-roll and serve.

Serves 6

Stuffed peppers

Medium-sized onion 1
Celery sticks 2
Mushrooms 4 oz (100 g)
Large tomato 1
Medium-sized carrot 1
Swede, or turnip or parsnip 4 oz (100 g)
Butter or margarine 1 oz (25 g)
Water ¼ pt (150 ml)
Tomato paste 1 tsp (5 ml)
Yeast extract ½ tsp (2.5 ml)
Salt & pepper to taste
Medium-sized green or red peppers 4
100% wholemeal flour 2 tbsp (30 ml)
Cheddar cheese, grated 4 oz (100 g)

Chop the onion, celery, mushrooms, tomato, and dice the carrot and swede. Melt the butter and fry the onion, carrot, celery, swede and mushrooms together for 5 minutes. Stir in the tomato, water, tomato paste and yeast extract. Cover and simmer for 10–15 minutes, until just tender. Meanwhile, halve the peppers lengthways and remove the seeds, then steam for 10 minutes. Arrange in an ovenproof serving dish.

Drain the vegetables, reserving the cooking liquor. Fill the peppers with the vegetables. Sprinkle the flour into the vegetable liquor and bring to the boil. Adjust seasoning to taste. Pour over the peppers, sprinkle with cheese and bake in the oven at 200°C (400°F/Mark 6) for 15 minutes. Serve at once.

Serves 4

Cheese, onion & tomato flan

The classic Cranks cheese flan – use leeks, mushrooms, courgettes or other vegetables to ring the changes

Wholemeal shortcrust pastry (*see page 230*) 8 oz (225 g)
Medium-sized onion 1
Butter or margarine 1 oz (25 g)
Cheddar cheese, grated 4 oz (100 g)
Free-range eggs 2
Milk ⅓ pt (200 ml)
French mustard 1 tsp (5 ml)
Salt & pepper to taste
Large tomato 1

Roll out the pastry and use to line a 7½" (19 cm) flan tin. Chop the onion. Melt the butter and sauté the onion until transparent. Allow to cool slightly, then sprinkle over the base of the flan. Sprinkle cheese on top. Beat the eggs, milk, mustard, salt and pepper together and pour into the flan case. Arrange the sliced tomato around the outside edge and bake in the oven at 180°C (350°F/Mark 4) for 40–45 minutes, until set and golden.

Serves 6

Stuffed aubergines

Medium-sized aubergines 2
Large onion 1
Butter or margarine 2 oz (50 g)
Mushrooms 6 oz (175 g)

Garlic clove, crushed 1
Parsley, chopped 3 tbsp (45 ml)
Cheddar cheese, grated 4 oz (100 g)
Salt & pepper to taste

Cut the aubergines in half lengthways and scoop out the flesh leaving a ½" (1.5 cm) 'wall'. Sprinkle the 'shells' with salt and leave to one side. Roughly chop the aubergine pulp and chop the onion and mushrooms. Melt the butter and sauté the aubergine and onion until the onion is transparent. Add the mushrooms and continue cooking for a further two minutes. Off the heat, stir in the remaining ingredients. Wash and dry the aubergine 'shells'. Place in a greased ovenproof dish and spoon in the filling. Pour over 4 tbsp (60 ml) water, cover and bake in the oven at 190°C (375°F/Mark 5) for about 45 minutes until tender and golden brown.

Serves 2–4

Homity pies

A good old English country recipe – one of the most popular at Cranks

Wholemeal shortcrust pastry (*see page 230*) 10 oz (300 g)
Potatoes ¾ lb (350 g)
Onions 1 lb (450 g)
Oil 3 tbsp (45 ml)
Butter or margarine 1 oz (25 g)
Parsley, chopped ½ oz (15 g)
Cheese, grated 4 oz (100 g)
Garlic cloves, crushed 2
Milk 1 tbsp (15 ml)
Salt & pepper to taste

Roll out the pastry and use to line six 4" (10 cm) individual tins or foil dishes. Boil or steam the potatoes until tender. Chop the onions, then sauté in the oil until really soft. Combine the potatoes and onions, add the butter, parsley, 2 oz (50 g) cheese, garlic, milk, and season well to taste. Cool, then use to fill the pastry cases. Sprinkle with the remaining cheese

and bake in the oven at 220°C (425°F/Mark 7) for 20 minutes,
until golden.

   Alternatively, use to make one 8″ (20 cm) flan. Bake for
25–30 minutes.

Makes 6 pies

Crécy plate pie

*Served hot or cold, this moist carrot filling complements the crisp
texture of the wholemeal pastry*

Onions 12 oz (350 g)
Carrots 12 oz (350 g)
Butter or margarine 2 oz (50 g)
Thyme 1 tsp (5 ml)
100% wholemeal flour 2 tbsp (30 ml)
Yeast extract 1 tsp (5 ml)
Salt & pepper to taste
Wholemeal shortcrust pastry (*see page 230*) 15 oz (425 g)

Chop the onions and grate the carrots. Melt the butter and
sauté the onion until transparent. Add the carrots and thyme
and simmer gently, stirring frequently, for 10 minutes. Stir in
the flour and yeast extract and season to taste. Leave to cool.

   Roll out a generous half of the pastry and use to line an 8″
(20 cm) pie plate or flan tin. Fill with the vegetable mixture,
then top with the remaining pastry. Seal the edges and flute
them. Make two slashes in the centre of the pie and bake in the
oven at 200°C (400°F/Mark 6) for about ½ hour, until golden.
Serve warm or cold.

Serves 6

Crispy mushroom layer

Wholemeal breadcrumbs 8 oz (225 g)
Mixed milled nuts 4 oz (100 g)
Butter or margarine 4 oz (100 g)
Large onion 1
Mushrooms 8 oz (225 g)

Tomatoes 8 oz (225 g)
Salt & pepper to taste
Marjoram 1 tsp (5 ml)

Combine the breadcrumbs and nuts. Melt 3 oz (75 g) butter and fry the bread and nut mixture together until golden. Chop the onion, mushrooms and tomatoes, then melt the remaining butter and sauté the onion until transparent. Add the remaining ingredients and simmer gently for 5 minutes. In a lightly greased ovenproof dish layer up the breadcrumbs and vegetables, starting and finishing with a layer of the bread and nut mixture. Bake in the oven at 190°C (375°F/Mark 5) for ½ hour.

Serves 4–6

Aubergine & red bean stew

A rich and hearty stew to keep out the winter cold

Red beans 8 oz (225 g)
Water 1½ pt (900 ml)
Large onions 2
Butter or margarine 2 oz (50 g)
Large aubergine 1
Tomatoes 8 oz (225 g)
Garlic clove, crushed 2
Tomato paste 2 tbsp (30 ml)
Vegetable stock cube 1
Basil 1 tsp (5 ml)
Salt & pepper to taste

WARNING: the red beans must boil vigorously for at least 10 minutes.

Soak the beans overnight. Drain, cover with fresh water and bring to the boil, making sure that they boil for at least 10 minutes, and simmer for 45 minutes. Chop the onions and tomatoes and dice the aubergine. Melt the butter and sauté the onions until transparent. Add the aubergine and continue cooking for a further 5 minutes, stirring occasionally. Add the beans with their cooking liquid and remaining ingredients. Cover and simmer for about 45 minutes, until the beans are tender. Add extra vegetable stock as required.

Serves 4–6

Country pasties

Cheese provides protein in these traditional pasties, which are ideal for school lunches and picnics

Mixed root vegetables (onion, turnip, carrot, potato) 8 oz (225 g)
Cheddar cheese, grated 4 oz (100 g)
Sage 1 tsp (5 ml)
Salt ½ tsp (2.5 ml)
Pepper ¼ tsp (1.25 ml)
Oil 2 tsp (10 ml)
Wholemeal shortcrust pastry (*see page 230*) 15 oz (425 g)

Combine the first 6 ingredients in a mixing bowl. Roll out the pastry on a lightly floured surface and cut out four 7″ (18 cm) rounds. Brush the edges with water. Spoon the filling into the centre of each and bring the edges up to form a pasty. Seal the edges well. Place on a baking sheet and bake in the oven at 200°C (400°F/Mark 6) for 15 minutes, reduce heat to 170°C (325°F/Mark 3) and cook for a further 15–20 minutes, until the vegetables are tender when tested.

Makes 4 pasties

Vegetable crumble

Most people think only of sweet crumbles, but here is an exciting savoury crumble incorporating cheese, nuts and seeds in the topping, covering a mixture of vegetables which may be varied with the season

For the crumble topping
Butter or margarine 4 oz (100 g)
100% wholemeal flour 6 oz (175 g)

Cheddar cheese, grated 4 oz (100 g)
Mixed nuts, chopped 2 oz (50 g)
Sesame seeds 2 tbsp (30 ml)

Base
Mixed root vegetables (parsnip, turnip, potato,
    carrot, etc.) 1½ lb (675 g)
Large onion 1
Butter or margarine 2 oz
100% wholemeal flour 1 oz (25 g)
Tomatoes 8 oz (225 g)
Vegetable stock ½ pt (300 ml)
Milk ¼ pt (142 ml)
Parsley, chopped 3 tbsp (45 ml)
Salt & pepper to taste

Rub the butter into the flour until the mixture resembles fine
crumbs. Add the cheese, nuts and sesame seeds.

Chop the vegetables, then melt the butter in a large
saucepan and sauté the onion until transparent. Add the
prepared vegetables and cook over gentle heat, stirring occasionally, for 10 minutes. Stir in the flour, then add the
remaining ingredients. Bring to the boil, reduce heat, cover
and simmer for about 15 minutes, until the vegetables are just
tender. Transfer to an ovenproof dish. Press the crumble
topping over the vegetables and bake in the oven at 190°C
(375°F/Mark 5) for about ½ hour, until golden.

Serves 6

Cheese & millet croquettes

*Millet has quite a bland flavour which is greatly improved by
adding a variety of herbs and other seasonings. Cheese combines
particularly well to make these tasty croquettes*

Water 1½ pt (900 ml)
Mixed herbs ½ tsp (2.5 ml)
Basil ½ tsp (2.5 ml)
Cayenne pepper, pinch
Ground bayleaf, pinch

Millet 10 oz (300 g)
Oil 3 tbsp (45 ml)
Medium-sized onion 1
Small pepper (optional) 1
Garlic clove 1
Cheddar cheese 8 oz (225 g)
Chopped parsley 4 tbsp (60 ml)
Salt & pepper to taste
Beaten egg to coat
Wholemeal breadcrumbs to coat

Bring measured water and herbs to the boil, stir in the millet and simmer gently for about 25 minutes, stirring frequently until all the water is absorbed. Heat the oil, chop the onion, pepper and garlic, and sauté until the onion is transparent. Combine the millet, sautéed vegetables, grated cheese and parsley and season generously with salt and pepper. Leave to cool, then shape into 8 'cakes'. Dip in the beaten egg and breadcrumbs until evenly coated. Fry in deep or shallow fat until golden brown. Serve hot or cold.

Makes 8 croquettes

Leek & cheese flan

Wholemeal shortcrust pastry (*see page 230*) 10 oz (300 g)
Large leeks 2
Butter or margarine 1 oz (25 g)
Cayenne, large pinch
Ground nutmeg, large pinch
Free-range eggs 3
Milk 3 fl. oz (75 ml)
Soured cream 3 fl. oz (75 ml)
Salt, large pinch
Cheddar cheese, grated 6 oz (175 g)

Roll out the pastry on a lightly floured working surface and use to line a 9″ (23 cm) flan tin. Slice the leeks and clean them thoroughly. Melt the butter and sauté the leeks until just tender. Season generously with cayenne and nutmeg. Leave to cool. Whisk the eggs, milk, soured cream and salt together. Sprinkle half the cheese over the base of the flan. Spread the leeks on top and sprinkle with the remaining cheese. Pour the egg custard into the flan case. Bake in the oven at 200°C (400°F/Mark 6) for about ½ hour until risen and golden. Serve warm or cold.

Serves 4–6

Puddings & Desserts

Many will undoubtedly say that a pudding or a sweet at the end of a meal is as unnecessary as a starter at the beginning. Certainly most health-conscious people will settle for a simple form of fruit or perhaps a yoghourt to complete a meal. Cranks, not wanting to go too far down the road of puritanism, prefers to subscribe to the view that 'a little of what you fancy does you good'.

Just for a moment, consider your favourite pudding recipe and then imagine it transformed with all the goodness of natural wholefood ingredients – fresh dairy cream, free-range eggs, raw sugar, 100% wholemeal flour – and you have Cranks daily fare!

Creamy yoghourt flan

The combination of natural yoghourt and soft cheeses gives this flan a delicate flavour. Make the plain one first, then try the variations

Wholemeal shortcrust pastry (*see page 230*) 6 oz (175 g)
Skimmed milk powder 2 oz (50 g)
Curd cheese 6 oz (175 g)
Cream cheese 6 oz (175 g)
Natural yoghourt ¼ pt (142 ml)
Clear honey 3 tbsp (45 ml)
Ground nutmeg or cinnamon

Roll out the pastry and use to line an 8″ (20 cm) fluted flan ring. Bake blind at 200°C (400°F/Mark 6) for 15 minutes. Meanwhile, blend together the milk powder, curd and cream cheese, natural yoghourt and honey until smooth. Pour the blended mixture into the warm pastry case, sprinkle with the ground spices and return to the oven for 15 minutes. Allow to cool in the tin, then refrigerate until set.

VARIATIONS
Citrus pie Pare the rind from 1 lemon, cut away all the white pith, then roughly chop the flesh, removing any pips. Add the rind and lemon flesh to the ingredients and blend together in a

liquidizer goblet until smooth. *Omit the spices.* Decorate with half slices of lemon.

Cinnamon pie Stir 2 oz (50 g) sultanas and 1 tsp (5 ml) ground cinnamon into the blended mixture.

Sunshine pie Repeat as for CITRUS PIE above, but substitute 1 small orange for lemon. Decorate with half slices of orange.

Serves 4–6

Banana yoghourt flan

Cooked banana has a natural sweetness and distinctive flavour to contrast with the sharpness of natural yoghourt and orange

Wholemeal shortcrust pastry (*see page 230*) 6 oz (175 g)
Bananas 6
Natural yoghourt ¼ pt (142 ml)
Orange, grated rind of ½

Roll out the pastry and use to line an 8″ (20 cm) fluted flan ring. Mash the bananas and beat in 4 tbsp (60 ml) yoghourt. Pour the banana mixture into the flan case. Spoon the remaining yoghourt through the mixture to give a decorative effect. Sprinkle with orange rind. Bake in the oven at 200°C (400°F/Mark 6) for 25–30 minutes. Cool in the tin. Serve cold.

Serves 4–6

Puréed fruit jelly

A real jelly!

Bananas 2
Dessert apple 1
Stoned dates 2 oz (50 g)
Apple juice, freshly extracted or bottled (*see page 242*)
Agar-agar 2 tsp (10 ml)

Roughly chop the fruit. Put the bananas, apples and dates into a liquidizer goblet with ¼ pt (150 ml) apple juice. Blend until smooth. Make up to 1 pt (600 ml) with more apple juice. Place the purée in a saucepan, whisk in the agar-agar and cook over a gentle heat, stirring all the time until the agar-agar is dissolved. Bring to the boil. Pour into wetted 1 pt (600 ml) mould or individual dishes. Refrigerate until required. If wished, decorate with fresh whipped cream or soured cream.

Serves 4–6

Lemon cheesecake

This cheesecake is neither baked nor set with jelling compound. It relies on the weight of the ingredients to hold its shape, so chill well and handle with care

For the base
Digestive biscuits 4 oz (100 g)
Butter or margarine, melted 2 oz (50 g)

For the filling
Lemons 2
Raw brown sugar 4 oz (100 g)
Cream cheese 12 oz (350 g)
Curd cheese 12 oz (350 g)
Fresh double cream ¼ pt (142 ml)

Whipped cream, green grapes, or grated lemon rind to decorate

Finely crush the biscuits and stir into the butter. Press the biscuit mixture into the base of an 8″ (20 cm) loose-bottomed deep cake tin.

Grate the rind from the lemons and squeeze out the juice. Place in a basin with the sugar. Beat well. Slowly beat in the cheeses and continue beating until the mixture is smooth. Whip the cream until it holds its shape and fold in the cheese. Spread the cheese mixture over biscuit base and level the surface. Cover and refrigerate for several hours.

Turn the cheesecake out on to a serving plate. Decorate with whipped cream and grape halves or lemon rind.

Serves 6–8

Lemon meringue pie

A family favourite in a new guise

Wholemeal shortcrust pastry (*see page 230*) 6 oz (175 g)
Lemons, grated rind & juice of 2
Water ¼ pt (150 ml)
Set honey 3 oz (75 g)
Maize flour 3 tbsp (45 ml)
Free-range eggs, separated 2
Raw brown sugar (preferably pale) 3 oz (75 g)

Roll out the pastry and use to line an 8″ (20 cm) pie plate or
sandwich tin. Bake blind at 220°C (425°F/Mark 7) for about
15 minutes. In a saucepan mix together the lemon rind and
juice, water, honey and maize flour. Bring to the boil, stirring,
and cook until thickened. Off the heat, beat in the egg yolks.
Allow to cool before spooning into the pastry case. Stiffly
whisk the egg whites until they stand in peaks. Whisk in the
sugar a spoonful at a time until stiff. Spoon on to the lemon
filling and bake in the oven at 170°C (325°F/Mark 3) for about
20 minutes, until golden. Leave to cool before cutting.

Serves 6

Sticky prune cake

Prunes 4 oz (100 g)
Raw brown sugar 4 oz (100 g)
Vegetable oil 4 fl. oz (100 ml)
Free-range eggs 2
100% wholemeal flour 5 oz (150 g)
Bicarbonate of soda ½ tsp (2.5 ml)
Ground cinnamon 1 tsp (5 ml)
Mixed spice ½ tsp (2.5 ml)
Ground nutmeg ½ tsp (2.5 ml)
Ground cloves, pinch
Buttermilk 4 fl. oz (100 ml)

Topping
Raw brown sugar 2 oz (50 g)

Buttermilk 3 tbsp (45 ml)
Black molasses or honey 1 tbsp (15 ml)
Vanilla essence, few drops

Wash the prunes and place them in a saucepan. Just cover with water and bring to the boil. Simmer 10–15 minutes until just tender. Drain, remove the stones and roughly chop. In a basin, whisk together the sugar, oil and eggs until thick and smooth. Stir in the flour, bicarbonate of soda and spices. Beat well. Stir in the prunes and buttermilk. Pour the mixture into a greased and lined 9″ (23 cm) sandwich tin, and bake in the oven at 180°C (350°F/Mark 4) for about 30 minutes, until firm to the touch.

Warm the ingredients for topping together in a small saucepan. Prick the cake all over with a skewer and spoon the syrup over the top. Leave to cool in the tin. Cut in wedges. Serve with fresh or soured cream.

Serves 6–8

Raw sugar jam tart

Wholemeal shortcrust pastry (*see page 230*) 6 oz (150 g)
Raw sugar jam 8 tbsp (120 ml)

Roll out a generous two-thirds of the pastry and use to line an 8″ (20 cm) pie plate. Spread the jam over the base. Roll out the remaining pastry and cut into ½″ (1.5 cm) strips. Arrange in a lattice over the jam, pressing the ends of the strips to secure them. Neaten the edges of the tart with the prongs of a fork. Bake in the oven at 200°C (400°F/Mark 6) for 20–25 minutes, until the pastry is golden.

Serves 6

Baked egg custard

An unusual variation of the traditional egg custard

Free-range eggs 4
Milk 1 pt (568 ml)
Cashew nuts, finely ground 2 oz (50 g)

Raw brown sugar 1 oz (25 g)
Vanilla essence 1 tsp (5 ml)
Grated orange rind ½ tsp (2.5 ml)
Ground nutmeg ¼ tsp (1.25 ml)
Raisins 2 oz (50 g)

Whisk together eggs and milk, then stir in the remaining ingredients, except the raisins. Grease a shallow 2 pt (1 l) ovenproof dish with butter or margarine. Sprinkle raisins over the base and pour the egg custard into the dish. Place the dish in a deep baking tin and pour in water to within 1″ (2.5 cm) of the top. Bake in the oven at 180°C (350°F/Mark 4) for about 1 hour until just set. Serve warm or cold.

Serves 4–6

Orange & banana trifle

Milk 1 pt (568 ml)
Raw brown sugar 2 tbsp (30 ml)
Free-range eggs 4
Vanilla essence ½ tsp (2.5 ml)
Arrowroot 1 tbsp (15 ml)
Left-over sponge cake 12 oz (350 g)
Oranges 3
Bananas, peeled and sliced 2
Fresh double cream, whipped ½ pt (284 ml)
Flaked almonds, toasted 1 oz (25 g)

Heat the milk and sugar in a saucepan to just below boiling point. Beat the eggs, vanilla essence and arrowroot together in a basin, then whisk in the milk. Return the custard to the saucepan and cook over a very gentle heat, stirring continuously until the custard thickens enough to coat the back of a wooden spoon. Remove from the heat at once.

Slice the sponge cake and place in the base of a serving dish. Remove the skin and white pith from the oranges and chop them, reserving the juice. Spoon the juice over the sponge, then arrange the oranges and bananas on top. Pour the warm custard over the fruit, cover and refrigerate until required.

Decorate with whipped cream and flaked almonds before serving.

Serves 8

Creamy bran & apple chunks

This is so quick to make, yet tastes delicious

Small dessert apples 2
Soured cream ¼ pt (142 ml)
Milk 2 tbsp (30 ml)
Walnuts, chopped 1 oz (25 g)
Thin honey 1–2 tbsp (15–30 ml)
Bran 3 tbsp (45 ml)
Apple slices 8

Finely chop the apples. Mix the soured cream and milk together in a basin. Stir in the remaining ingredients and transfer to individual serving dishes. Decorate with apple slices.

 If this dessert is kept in the refrigerator for several days it will tend to thicken. Thin to the required consistency with a little milk.

VARIATIONS
Carob and apple Omit walnuts and add 3 tbsp (30 ml) of carob powder.

Orange and nut Substitute 2 small peeled oranges or mandarins for the apples, and add a little grated orange or lemon rind.

Serves 4

Apple pie

Cooking apples 2 lb (900 g)
Water 1 tbsp (15 ml)
Raw brown sugar 2 oz (50 g)
Lemon, grated rind of ½
Ground cloves ¼ tsp (1.25 ml)
Wholemeal shortcrust pastry (*see page 230*) 15 oz (450 g)

Wipe, core and slice the apples, then place the apples, water, sugar, lemon rind and cloves in a saucepan. Simmer for 10 minutes, stirring occasionally. Do not allow the apple to become 'pulpy'. Leave to cool.

Roll out pastry and use a generous half to line a 9" (23 cm) pie plate. Fill with apple. Use the remaining pastry to top the pie. Seal the edges well, make a hole in the centre, then flute to give a decorative edge. Bake in the oven at 200°C (400°F/Mark 6) for about 25 minutes, until golden. Serve warm or cold.

Serves 6

Bakewell tart

An old English classic in the Cranks style

Wholemeal shortcrust pastry (*see page 230*) 6 oz (175 g)
Jam 4 tbsp (60 ml)
Raw brown sugar 3 oz (75 g)
Butter or margarine 3 oz (75 g)
Free-range eggs, beaten 2
Almond essence ½ tsp (2.5 ml)
Soya flour 2 oz (50 g)
Baking powder ½ tsp (2.5 ml)
Flaked almonds 3 tbsp (45 ml)

Roll out the pastry and use it to line an 8" (20 cm) sandwich tin or pie plate. Spread the base with jam. Cream the sugar and butter together until light and fluffy. Beat in the eggs a little at a time (if necessary add some soya flour to prevent curdling). Beat in the almond essence, soya flour and baking powder. Spread the mixture carefully over the jam. Sprinkle flaked almonds on top and bake in the oven at 170°C (325°F/Mark 3) for about 1 hour, until risen and golden.

Serves 4–6

Spiced bread pudding

A clever way to use stale bread to make a lovely pudding

Stale wholemeal bread 8 oz (225 g)
Milk ½ pt (284 ml)
Currants, sultanas & raisins, mixed 4 oz (100 g)
Butter or margarine, grated 2 oz (50 g)
Raw brown sugar 4 oz (100 g)
Ground mixed spice 1 tbsp (15 ml)
Free-range egg 1
Milk 4 tbsp (60 ml)
Ground nutmeg, pinch

Roughly break up the bread and place it in a mixing bowl with the milk. Leave to soak. Add the dried fruits, butter, sugar and mixed spice. Beat well. Whisk together the egg and milk and add to the bread mixture. Turn into a greased shallow ovenproof dish, level the surface, and sprinkle with ground nutmeg. Bake in the oven at 180°C (350°F/Mark 4) for about 45 minutes, until set. Serve hot or cold.

Serves 6

Tangy apple swirl

Cooking apples 1 lb (450 g)
Butter or margarine 1 oz (25 g)
Raw brown sugar 2 oz (50 g)
Ground cloves, pinch
Lemon, grated rind of ½
Natural yoghourt ½ pt (284 ml)

Peel, core and chop the apples. Place all the ingredients, except yoghourt, in a saucepan. Cook over gentle heat, stirring occasionally, until the apples are 'pulpy'. Stir thoroughly to give a 'rough' purée. Leave to cool. In a glass serving dish, or individual dishes, spoon alternate spoonfuls of yoghourt and apple until it is all used up. With a knife, swirl the mixtures to give a decorative effect. Serve chilled.

Serves 4

Grape & banana flan

A special occasion flan with a rich pastry base

Pastry
100% wholemeal flour 4 oz (100 g)
Egg yolks 2
Butter or margarine, softened 2 oz (50 g)
Raw brown sugar 2 oz (50 g)

Filling
Egg yolks 2
100% wholemeal flour 1 oz (25 g)
Cornmeal 2 tbsp (30 ml)
Raw brown sugar 1 oz (25 g)
Milk ½ pt (284 ml)
Lemon, grated rind of ½

Topping
Banana 1
Lemon, juice of ½
Black grapes, halved & pips removed 6 oz (175 g)
Apricot jam 2 tbsp (30 ml)

For the pastry
Put the flour in a basin, and make a well in the centre. Put the egg yolks, butter and sugar in the centre and work them together drawing the flour in with the fingertips, to give a soft, manageable dough. Roll out on a lightly floured surface and use to line a 7½" (19 cm) fluted flan ring. Prick the base, chill for ½ hour, then bake blind at 190°C (375°F/Mark 5) for about 20 minutes. Leave to cool. Remove from tin.

For the filling
Put the egg yolks, flour, cornmeal, sugar and a little milk into a basin and mix to a smooth paste. Heat the milk, then pour over the egg mixture, stirring all the time. Return to the pan and cook over gentle heat, stirring until thickened. Off the heat, stir in the lemon rind. Cover and leave to cool. Spread over the base of the flan.

For the topping
Peel and slice the banana, dip in lemon juice, drain, reserving the juice. Arrange a circle of grape halves, then one of banana slices on top of the flan. Repeat until the fruit is used up. Mix apricot jam and lemon juice in a saucepan. Heat gently, then brush over the fruit to glaze. Chill until required.

ALTERNATIVE
Strawberry flan Use ½ lb (225 g) strawberries and 2 tbsp (30 ml) strawberry jam for the glaze.

Serves 6

Junket

Served with stewed fruit, this is an ideal dessert for all the family, although it has been regarded as an invalid delicacy in the past

Fresh milk 1 pt (568 ml)
Raw brown sugar 1 tsp (5 ml)
Vegetarian rennet 1 tsp (5 ml)
Ground nutmeg

Heat the milk and sugar in a saucepan to 45°C (110°F). Off the heat, stir in the rennet. Pour the milk into a serving dish. Sprinkle with nutmeg and leave to cool.
   If you do not have a thermometer, test the milk with the tip of a finger. The milk should feel 'comfortably' hot.

Serves 4

'Toffeed' rhubarb fool

Rhubarb 1 lb (450 g)
Pale, raw brown sugar 2 oz (50 g)
Butter or margarine 2 oz (50 g)
Fresh double cream ½ pt (284 ml)

Trim and slice the rhubarb then put the rhubarb, sugar and butter in a saucepan over gentle heat until the butter melts. Simmer gently until the rhubarb is 'pulpy' and thick, stirring occasionally. Chill until cold. Whip the cream until it holds its shape, then fold in the rhubarb. Spoon into individual glass dishes. Serve chilled.

Serves 4–6

Custard tart

Wholemeal shortcrust pastry (*see page 230*) 9 oz (225 g)
Free-range eggs 2
Milk ½ pt (284 ml)
Raw brown sugar ½ oz (15 g)
Ground nutmeg

Roll out the pastry and use it to line a 7″ (18 cm) flan tin. Whisk together the eggs, milk and sugar and pour into the pastry case. Sprinkle generously with ground nutmeg and bake in the oven at 190°C (375°F/Mark 5) for about 25 minutes, until lightly set. Leave to cool in the tin.

Serves 4–6

Walnut pie

Deliciously rich and sticky, this rather expensive recipe can be kept for a special treat

Wholemeal shortcrust pastry (*see page 230*) 15 oz (425 g)
Shelled walnuts, roughly chopped 8 oz (225 g)
Fresh double cream 4 fl. oz (100 ml)
Clear honey 4 fl. oz (100 ml)
Free-range eggs 3
Raw brown sugar 4 oz (100 g)

Roll out a generous half of the pastry and use it to line a 9½″ (24 cm) flan tin or sandwich tin. Sprinkle the walnuts over the base. Whisk together the remaining ingredients and pour carefully over the walnuts. Roll out the remaining pastry and use it to top the pie. Seal well at the edges. Bake in the oven at 200°C (400°F/Mark 6) for 15 minutes, reduce heat to 180°C (350°F/Mark 4) and cook for a further 25 minutes. Leave until cold before cutting. Serve with fresh or soured cream.

Serves 6

Hazelnut & black cherry tart

100% wholemeal flour 3 oz (75 g)
Ground cinnamon ½ tsp (2.5 ml)
Raw brown sugar 3 oz (75 g)
Hazelnuts, finely ground 3 oz (75 g)
Lemon, grated rind of ½
Unsalted butter 4 oz (100 g)
Egg yolks 2
Vanilla essence ¼ tsp (1.25 ml)
Black cherry jam 12 oz (350 g)
Beaten egg 1 tbsp (15 ml)
Soured cream 1 tbsp (15 ml)

In a basin, combine the first 5 ingredients. Rub in the butter until the mixture resembles breadcrumbs. Add the egg yolks and vanilla essence and work together to give a soft dough. Wrap in greaseproof paper or cling-film and chill for at least 30 minutes. On a lightly floured surface, roll out three-quarters of the 'pastry' and use to line an 8″ (20 cm) loose-bottomed flan tin or sandwich tin. (The pastry may crack a little; if it does, simply press it into the tin.) Spread the jam over the base of the pastry. Use the remaining pastry to make strips for the top of the tart. Lay them across the top of the jam in a lattice effect. Neaten the edges. Beat together the beaten egg and soured cream and carefully brush the pastry with it. Bake in the oven at 180°C (350°F/Mark 4) for about 40 minutes until crisp and golden on the top. Leave to go completely cold before removing from the tin and serving.

Serves 6

Carrageen citrus jelly

Carrageen has a unique flavour which permeates this jelly and gives it a dark opaque look

Water 1 pt (600 ml)
Carrageen 1 oz (25 g)
Lemons 2

Orange 1
Raw pale brown sugar 4 oz (100 g)
Green grapes to decorate

Put the water and carrageen in a saucepan. Pare the rind from the lemons and orange and add it to the pan. Bring to the boil, then simmer for 15 minutes. Squeeze the juice from the fruits. Add to the hot liquid. Put the sugar in a basin, strain the hot liquid over the sugar, stirring until it dissolves. Pour into a serving dish and leave until set. Decorate with grape halves.

Serves 4

Devon apple cake

This traditional Devon recipe, first introduced into Cranks restaurant at Dartington in Devon, should of course always be served with clotted cream!

100% wholemeal self-raising flour 8 oz (225 g)
Salt ¼ tsp (1.25 ml)
Ground cinnamon 1 tsp (5 ml)
Mixed spice 1 tsp (5 ml)
Raw brown sugar 4 oz (100 g)
Butter or margarine 4 oz (100 g)
Cooking apples 12 oz (350 g)
Free-range egg, beaten 1

Grease and line the base of a 7½" (19 cm) square cake tin. In a basin combine the flour, salt, cinnamon, mixed spice and sugar. Rub in the butter or margarine until the mixture resembles fine crumbs. Wash, core and roughly chop the apples, then add the apples and beaten egg to the mixture and stir quickly to combine. Spread evenly in the tin and bake in the oven at 190°C (375°F/Mark 5) for about ½ hour, until risen and firm to the touch. Allow to cool in the tin before cutting into squares.

Serves about 6

Carob blancmange

An old favourite, using carob instead of chocolate powder

Carob powder 3 tbsp (45 ml)
Raw brown sugar 3 tbsp (45 ml)
Gelozone jelling compound 1 tbsp (15 ml)
Water 3 tbsp (45 ml)
Milk 1 pt (568 ml)
Whipped cream to decorate
Carob bar to decorate

In a basin, mix together the carob powder, sugar, Gelozone and cold water to a smooth paste. Heat the milk to just below boiling and pour over the carob paste, stirring all the time. Return to the saucepan and simmer for 2 minutes, stirring continuously. Pour into a wetted 1 pt (600 ml) mould. Chill until set. Unmould and decorate with whipped cream and grated carob bar.

Serves 4–6

Brandied prune mousse

Prunes 8 oz (225 g)
Brandy 1 tbsp (15 ml)
Fresh double cream 4 fl. oz (100 ml)
Egg whites 2

Cover the prunes with water and allow to soak overnight. Bring to the boil, reduce heat, cover and simmer for about 15 minutes until really soft. Drain, reserving the juice, and leave to cool. Discard the stones and blend the prunes in a liquidizer goblet, using about 4 tbsp (60 ml) of the reserved juice, until the prunes are a thick purée. Stir in the brandy. Whip the cream until it just holds its shape. Stiffly whisk the egg whites. Fold the whipped cream and then the egg whites into the prune purée. Spoon into a serving dish or individual dishes. Cover and chill until required.

Serves 6

Buttermilk dessert

This dessert has an intriguing flavour and texture to keep friends guessing!

Pumpernickel, grated 8 oz (225 g)
Buttermilk ¾ pt (426 ml)
Lemon, grated rind of 1
Set honey 3 tbsp (45 ml)
Raisins 2 oz (50 g)
Vanilla essence 1 tsp (5 ml)

Mix all the ingredients together. Cover and chill until required. Serve in individual glass dishes.

This mixture will thicken on standing. Thin with extra buttermilk, as required.

Serves 6

Honey & apple tart

Medium-sized cooking apples 2 (about 12 oz/350 g)
Honey ¼ pt (150 ml)
Lemon, juice & rind of 1
Fresh wholemeal breadcrumbs 6 oz (175 g)
Wholemeal shortcrust pastry (*see page 230*) 9 oz (250 g)

Grate the apples and mix together with the honey, lemon rind and juice, and the breadcrumbs. Roll out the pastry on a lightly floured surface and use to line an 8″ (20 cm) flan tin. Spoon the filling in the centre, level the surface and bake in the oven at 200°C (400°F/Mark 6) for 30–35 minutes, until firm to the touch. Serve warm or cold.

Serves 4–6

Date & apple squares

Cooking apples 1 lb (450 g)
Shelled walnuts 2 oz (50 g)
Stoned dates 4 oz (100 g)

100% wholemeal self-raising flour 4 oz (100 g)
Raw brown sugar 4 oz (100 g)
Clear honey 1 tbsp (15 ml)
Butter or margarine, melted 1 oz (25 g)
Free-range egg 1
Salt, pinch

Dice the apples, chop the walnuts and dates, and place in a basin with all the remaining ingredients. Mix well to combine evenly, then spread the mixture into a lightly greased 8″ (20 cm) square shallow tin. Bake in the oven at 200°C (400°F/Mark 6) for about ½ hour until golden and risen. Cut into squares and serve warm with fresh or soured cream.

Serves 4–6

Treacle tart

Instead of the usual syrup filling, the Cranks special recipe uses a mixture of black treacle and honey lightened with coconut

Black treacle ¼ pt (150 ml)
Honey ¼ pt (150 ml)
Lemon, grated rind of ½
Desiccated coconut 3 oz (75 g)
Fresh wholemeal breadcrumbs 3 oz (75 g)
Wholemeal shortcrust pastry (*see page 230*) 9 oz (250 g)

Combine the first 5 ingredients and stir well until evenly mixed. On a lightly floured surface roll out the pastry and use it to line an 8″ (20 cm) flan ring or tin. Pour the filling in the centre and bake in the oven at 200°C (400°F/Mark 6) for 30–35 minutes, until the pastry is golden. Leave to cool in the tin. Serve with ice-cream or soured cream.

Serves 6

Apple crumble

Cooking apples 1½ lb (675 g)
Water 3 tbsp (45 ml)

Raw brown sugar 4 oz (100 g)
Mixed spice 1 tsp (5 ml)

For the crumble
Butter or margarine 3 oz (75 g)
100% wholemeal flour 6 oz (175 g)

Wipe, core and slice the apples, then place the apples, water, half the sugar and mixed spice in a saucepan and simmer gently for about 10 minutes. Do not allow the apples to become 'pulpy'. Place the apple mixture in a 2 pt (1.2 l) ovenproof dish. Leave to cool.

Rub the butter into the flour until the mixture resembles fine crumbs. Stir in the remaining sugar. Press the crumble topping on to the apples. Bake in the oven at 200°C (400°F/Mark 6) for 20–25 minutes. Serve warm.

Serves 4

Bread & butter pudding

Thin slices of wholemeal bread 4 (about 4 oz/100 g)
Butter or margarine 1 oz (25 g)
Raw brown sugar 1 tbsp (15 ml)
Mixed sultanas, raisins & currants 2 oz (50 g)
Fresh milk ¾ pt (426 ml)
Free-range eggs 2
Ground cinnamon ¼ tsp (1.25 ml)
Nutmeg ¼ tsp (1.25 ml)

Cut 4 thin slices of wholemeal bread, preferably stale bread. Spread the bread with butter or margarine, cut each piece into quarters. Arrange half of the bread, buttered side up, on the base of a 1½ pt (900 ml) ovenproof dish. Sprinkle with half the sugar and dried fruit. Repeat the layer once more. Whisk together the milk, eggs and spices. Pour the custard over the bread. Bake in the oven at 180°C (350°F/Mark 4) for about 45 minutes until just set. Serve hot.

Serves 6

Baked apples

A recipe often overlooked. Choose best quality apples for good results

Medium-sized cooking apples 4
Raw brown sugar 1 oz (25 g)
Sultanas or raisins 2 oz (50 g)
Whole cloves 8
Butter or margarine 1 oz (25 g)
Clear honey 2 tbsp (30 ml)
Water 2 tbsp (30 ml)

Wipe and core the apples. Score a line around the centre of each apple. Place the apples in an ovenproof dish allowing a little space between each one. Combine the sugar and sultanas and use to fill the centre. Press 2 cloves into the centre of each apple, dot with butter. Spoon the honey, then the water, over the apples. Bake in the oven at 200°C (400°F/Mark 6) for 30–45 minutes, until tender. Serve with fresh or soured cream or with EGG CUSTARD (*see page 154*).

Serves 4

Pouding Alsace

A superior version of Eve's pudding, with a delicious flavour and light texture

Cooking apples 1 lb (450 g)
Butter or margarine 3 oz (75 g)
Apricot jam 2 oz (50 g)
Raw brown sugar 3 oz (75 g)
Free-range eggs, separated 3
Fresh wholemeal breadcrumbs 2 oz (50 g)
100% wholemeal self-raising flour ½ oz (15 g)
Cinnamon 1 tsp (5 ml)

Core and slice the apples. Melt 1 oz (25 g) of butter in a saucepan, add the apples and cook over gentle heat for about 5 minutes. Do not allow them to go 'pulpy'. Off the heat, stir in the jam and turn the mixture into a greased ovenproof serving dish. Cream the remaining butter and sugar together until light and fluffy. Beat in the egg yolks. Combine breadcrumbs, flour and cinnamon. Stiffly whisk the egg whites. Fold the dry ingredients, then the egg whites, into the creamed mixture. Spoon over the apples and level the surface. Bake in the oven at 170°C (325°F/Mark 3) for about 40 minutes until the sponge is set and golden.

Serves 6

Mincemeat & apple 'jalousie'

A very special dessert, with an exciting filling – it was first tried out in Cranks in Dartington where we discovered that clotted cream is a 'must' with it, especially when making the dessert for a special occasion

Cooking apples 8 oz (225 g)
Wholemeal shortcrust pastry (*see page 230*) 1 quantity
Mincemeat 8 oz (225 g)
Beaten egg to glaze
Flaked almonds 3 tbsp (45 ml)
Clear honey 2 tbsp (30 ml)

Wash, core and roughly chop the apples. Add 1 tbsp (15 ml) water and cook over gentle heat for about 10 minutes until just soft. Cool. Roll out the pastry on a lightly floured surface to an oblong 18 × 7" (45 × 18 cm). Trim the edges and cut in half to give two oblongs 9 × 7" (23 × 18 cm). Flour one oblong lightly and fold in half lengthwise. Using a sharp knife, cut a series of slits through the pastry about ½" (1.5 cm) apart, and to within 1" (2.5 cm) of the edges. Unfold to give a 'shuttered' effect.

Put the plain oblong of pastry on a greased baking sheet and spread mincemeat down the centre. Spoon the apple down both sides of the mincemeat to within 1" (2.5 cm) of the edge. Dampen the edges of the pastry and carefully place the second piece of pastry on the top. Seal the edges well, then flute to give a decorative edge. Brush with beaten egg, sprinkle with flaked almonds and bake in the oven at 220°C (425°F/Mark 7) for 20–25 minutes, until golden. While still warm, brush with honey. Serve warm or cold.

Serves 4–6

Home-made yoghourt

Making yoghourt at home is very easy and fun too. Buy a carton of natural yoghourt to begin with, but once you have made a batch of yoghourt, keep a tablespoonful to use as a 'starter' for the next batch.

Fresh milk is the most popular base, but yoghourt can be made entirely from reconstituted skimmed milk – which cuts down on calories for those trying to watch their weight. Follow the instructions on the tin for reconstituting the powder, then proceed as with fresh milk.

Natural yoghourt may be served on its own, with fresh or stewed fruit, or honey, stirred into soups and stews, and used in baking.

Chopped or puréed fruits, raw sugar jams, grated carob or savoury flavourings, such as tomato juice, finely chopped herbs, and grated vegetables, may be added to natural yoghourt.

Fresh cow or goat milk 1 pt (568 ml)
Natural yoghourt 1 tbsp (15 ml)
Skimmed milk powder (optional) 1–2 tbsp (15–30 ml)

Preheat a heatproof dish and a well fitting lid, or thermos flask, with boiling water. Heat milk to 'blood' heat: 37°C (98°F). Put yoghourt into a basin and stir in the milk powder, if used. Pour a little of the warm milk on to the yoghourt, stir well, then pour the yoghourt into the pan of milk. Stir well again, then pour into the warmed dish and cover with the lid. Cover the container with a thick cloth and leave in a warm place, such as an airing cupboard, overnight, until the milk clots.

If a thermos flask is used, it is, of course, not necessary to leave it in a warm place, so this is probably the most convenient method.

Serves 4

Christmas pudding

A rich, dark and fruity pudding – made every year at Cranks Dartington Branch and sold in all the Cranks shops

Wholemeal breadcrumbs 6 oz (175 g)
100% wholemeal flour 3 oz (75 g)
Currants 8 oz (225 g)
Raisins 8 oz (225 g)
Sultanas 8 oz (225 g)
Almonds, chopped 1 oz (25 g)
Raw brown sugar 8 oz (225 g)
Ground mixed spice ½ tsp (2.5 ml)
Ground nutmeg ¼ tsp (1.25 ml)
Nutter 6 oz (175 g)
Free-range eggs 3
Raw sugar marmalade 1 tbsp (15 ml)
Sherry 4 fl. oz (100 ml)
Lemon, grated rind of ½

Thoroughly combine all the dry ingredients together in a large mixing bowl. Melt the Nutter, beat the eggs, and add all the remaining ingredients to the bowl. Stir well until evenly mixed. Grease 2 pudding basins and press the mixture into them. Cut 2 large circles of greaseproof paper – about 4" (10 cm) larger than the tops of the pudding basins – brush them with oil and make a pleat in each. Place over the basins and secure with string. Top with a piece of kitchen foil. Steam for 6 hours. Reheat by steaming for a further 1½ hours. Serve with fresh cream or a sweet sauce.

Makes two 1¾ lb (800 g) puddings

Cakes & Scones

It is very difficult to believe that Marie Antoinette, who must have been a reasonably intelligent woman, even though spoilt and over-privileged, can have made such a stupid remark as 'Well, let them eat cake' when told that the population of Paris were starving for the want of sufficient bread! But the story does highlight the position of cake as a luxury food, which it undoubtedly is.

So let us accept that we don't *need* cake, but that it can nevertheless be a very pleasant addition to a social tea time – and while we are about it, let us at least rob the occasion of the worst horrors of fattening and de-nourishing white flour, white sugar and chemically flavoured and coloured jams.

Again, there is a prejudice in the public mind that 100% wholemeal means 'heavy'. This is pure fallacy, and a visit to any Cranks to experience a piece of delicious light wholemeal sponge cake will prove the point.

Cake making needs to take place without hurry. All the ingredients should be taken out of the refrigerator long before starting so that they come up to room temperature. Each ingredient should then be carefully mixed and beaten into the mixture before adding the next. The more you enjoy making the cake the better the cake will be!

Belgian cake

This unusual cake with a surprisingly light texture is an ideal way to disguise left-over mincemeat in the New Year

Butter or margarine 4 oz (100 g)
Raw brown sugar 3 oz (75 g)
Free-range eggs, beaten 2
100% wholemeal self-raising flour 5 oz (150 g)
Raw sugar mincemeat 8 oz (225 g)
Water 1 tbsp (15 ml)

Cream the butter and sugar together until pale and fluffy. Beat in the eggs a little at a time. Fold in the flour, then fold in the mincemeat and water. Spoon the mixture into a greased and base-lined 8″ (20 cm) square shallow cake tin. Level the surface. Bake in the oven at 170°C (325°F/Mark 3) for about 30 minutes, until well risen and golden. Cool in the tin.

Old-fashioned ginger cake

100% wholemeal flour 8 oz (225 g)
Bicarbonate of soda ½ tsp (2.5 ml)
Ground ginger 2 tsp (10 ml)
Butter or margarine 4 oz (100 g)
Raw brown sugar 4 oz (100 g)
Black treacle or molasses 4 tbsp (60 ml)
Milk 2 tbsp (30 ml)
Free-range egg 1

Stir together the flour, bicarbonate of soda and ginger. Melt the butter in a saucepan with the sugar and treacle. Cool slightly, then beat in the milk and egg. Stir the liquid ingredients into the flour. Beat well, then turn into a greased and base-lined 900 g (2 lb) loaf tin. Bake in the oven at 180°C (350°F/Mark 4) for 40–45 minutes, until risen and firm to the touch. Cool on a wire tray.

100% Wholemeal sponge

The Cranks version of a whisked sponge recipe in which a high proportion of eggs to flour and sugar gives it a special texture

Free-range eggs 4
Vanilla essence ½ tsp (2.5 ml)
Raw brown sugar 1 oz (25 g)
100% wholemeal flour 1 oz (25 g)
Raw sugar jam or whipped cream to fill

Line two 7″ (18 cm) sandwich tins with non-stick silicone paper. Put the eggs, vanilla essence and sugar in a basin and whisk until really thick. Fold in the flour with a metal spoon or spatula. Divide the mixture between the tins, level the surface and bake in the oven at 180°C (350°F/Mark 4) for 15–20 minutes, until golden and firm to the touch. Cool slightly in the tin before transferring to a wire tray. When cold, sandwich together with jam and/or whipped cream. For special occasions, top with BROWN SUGAR ICING (*see page 178*).

Swiss roll

Free-range eggs 4
Vanilla essence ½ tsp (2.5 ml)
Raw brown sugar 1 oz (25 g)
100% wholemeal flour 1 oz (25 g)
Raw sugar jam 6 tbsp (90 ml)
Fresh double cream, whipped ¼ pt (142 ml)

Line a 7½ × 11½″ (19 × 29 cm) Swiss roll tin with non-stick silicone paper. Put the eggs, vanilla essence and sugar in the basin and whisk together until really thick – this will take 10–25 minutes, depending on whether you use an electric or a balloon whisk. Fold in the flour and pour the mixture into the prepared tin and level the surface. Bake in the oven at 180°C (350°F/Mark 4) for about 20 minutes, until golden brown and firm to the touch. Turn out carefully on to a piece of non-stick paper. Remove the lining paper from the cooked Swiss roll and, with a sharp knife, make an indentation about ½″ (1.5 cm) from one short edge. Starting at that edge, roll up the sponge with the paper in between and leave to cool. When cool, unroll and spread with jam and cream, then re-roll.

Christmas cake

A rich fruit cake which improves with keeping. This recipe can also be used for a wedding, birthday or other celebration cake

Raisins 2¼ lb (1 kg)
Currants 1 lb (450 g)
Stoned dates, chopped 6 oz (175 g)
Cooked prunes, stoned & chopped 4 oz (100 g)
Flaked almonds 8 oz (225 g)
Butter or margarine 14 oz (400 g)
Raw brown sugar 14 oz (400 g)
Free-range eggs 8
Lemon, grated rind of 1

Orange, grated rind of 1
Black treacle 1 tbsp (15 ml)
100% wholemeal flour 1 lb (450 g)
Salt 1 tsp (5 ml)
Ground nutmeg, allspice, cinnamon & ginger 1 tsp (5 ml)
  each
Sherry 5 tbsp (75 ml)

Grease and line a cake tin with a double thickness of grease-proof paper. Secure brown paper round the outside of the tin. Combine the raisins, currants, dates, prunes and almonds in a large basin. Cream the butter and sugar until pale and fluffy, then beat in the eggs one at a time. Stir in the lemon and orange rind and the black treacle. If there is any sign of curdling, stir in a spoonful of flour. Combine the flour, salt and spices and fold into the mixture alternately with the mixed fruits. Stir in the sherry. Turn the mixture into the prepared tin. Smooth the surface and bake in the oven at 150°C (300°F/Mark 2) for 1 hour. Reduce heat to 140°C (275°F/Mark 1) for a further 4 hours. Cover with greaseproof paper if the surface is overbrowning. Leave the cake to cool in its tin overnight, then remove from the tin and wrap in a double thickness of kitchen foil. Store in a cool dry place until required.

To decorate
Cover with 2 lb (900 g) almond paste or mock marzipan and icing (*see following three recipes*).

Makes 10" (25 cm) round or 9" (23 cm) square cake

Almond paste

Ground almonds 4 oz (100 g)
Raw pale brown sugar 4 oz (100 g)
Beaten egg 2 tbsp (30 ml)
Almond essence ½ tsp (2.5 ml)

Sift the ground almonds and sugar into a basin. Stir together the egg and almond essence and mix with the almonds to form a soft, manageable 'dough'.

Makes about ½ lb (225 g)

Mock marzipan

An alternative to almond paste for vegans

Raw pale brown sugar 10 oz (300 g)
Soya flour 4 oz (100 g)
Margarine, softened 2 oz (50 g)
Almond essence 1 tsp (5 ml)
Water 1–2 tbsp (15–30 ml)

Mix the dry ingredients together in a basin and rub in the margarine. Add the almond essence and sufficient water to mix to a soft, manageable 'dough'.

Makes about 1 lb (450 g)

Brown sugar icing

Raw pale brown sugar 4 oz (100 g)
Lemon juice 2 tbsp (30 ml)
Vanilla essence, few drops

Mill the sugar in a coffee grinder or pass it through a fine sieve. Add the lemon juice and vanilla essence and beat until smooth. Use to coat biscuits or the top of a cake.

Luscious lemon cake

A warm syrup is poured over the finished cake to give it an extra lemony flavour – quite irresistible!

Butter or margarine 4 oz (100 g)
Raw brown sugar 5 oz (150 g)
Lemon, grated rind & juice of 1
Free-range egg 1
100% wholemeal self-raising flour 4 oz (100 g)

Grease and line the base of a 7″ (18 cm) square tin. Heat the butter and 4 oz of the sugar over a gentle heat until the butter is melted. Off the heat, stir in the lemon rind. Whisk the egg in a basin, and then whisk it into the sugar mixture. Fold in the flour and turn the mixture into the prepared tin. Bake in the oven at 180°C (350°F/Mark 4) for about 30 minutes, until just firm to the touch. Warm the remaining 1 oz (25 g) sugar with the lemon juice. Prick the cake all over with a fork or wooden cocktail stick and spoon the syrup over the cake. Leave in the tin to cool. Cut into squares.

Carob cake

This cake just had to be included because of the continuing requests for the recipe from our customers

Butter or margarine 4 oz (100 g)
Raw brown sugar 4 oz (100 g)
Free-range eggs, separated 4
Vanilla essence ½ tsp (2.5 ml)
Almond essence ½ tsp (2.5 ml)
Carob powder 2 oz (50 g)
100% wholemeal flour 1½ oz (40 g)
Ground almonds 1½ oz (40 g)

Filling
Stoned prunes 3 oz (75 g)
Apricot jam 2 tbsp (30 ml)

Topping
Water 2 tbsp (30 ml)
Carob bar 2.8 oz (80 g)
Butter or margarine 1 oz (25 g)
Flaked almonds to decorate

Grease and line the base of two 7″ (18 cm) sandwich tins. Cream the butter and sugar until light and fluffy. Beat in the egg yolks and essences. Combine the carob powder, flour and ground almonds. Stiffly whisk the egg whites. Fold the dry ingredients and egg whites alternately into the mixture. Spoon the mixture into the prepared tins and level the surface. Bake in the oven at 180°C (350°F/Mark 4) for about 20 minutes, until just firm to the touch. Cool on a wire tray.

For the filling Place the prunes in a saucepan, just cover with water and simmer until tender. Drain, allow to cool, then remove the stones and roughly chop the prunes. Spread the apricot jam on one of the cakes, top with the prunes, then sandwich the two cakes together.

For the topping Place the water and the broken carob bar in a saucepan over a gentle heat, and stir until the carob is melted. Take off the heat and beat in the butter. Allow to cool slightly, then spread over the top of the cake. Decorate with a ring of flaked almonds round the edge.

Date & coconut gâteau

Butter or margarine 4 oz (100 g)
Raw brown sugar 4 oz (100 g)
Free-range eggs 2
100% wholemeal self-raising flour 3 oz (75 g)
Desiccated coconut 1 oz (25 g)

Filling
Stoned dates, chopped 4 oz (100 g)
Water 3 tbsp (45 ml)
Egg yolks 2
Raw brown sugar 1 oz (25 g)
Milk 2 tbsp (30 ml)
Arrowroot 1½ tsp (7.5 ml)
Butter or margarine 2 oz (50 g)

Topping
Desiccated coconut, toasted 2 oz (50 g)
Whole dates 4
Clear honey to glaze

Grease and line the base of two 7″ (18 cm) sandwich tins. Cream the butter and sugar until light and fluffy. Beat in the eggs, then fold in the flour and coconut. Turn the mixture into the prepared tins, level the surface, and bake in the oven at 180°C (350°F/Mark 4) for about 15 minutes, until just firm to the touch. Cool on a wire tray. Leave until cold.

For the filling Place the dates and water in a saucepan and simmer for 10–15 minutes until soft. Blend together the egg yolks, sugar, milk and arrowroot. Off the heat, stir the egg mixture into the dates and return to the heat. Simmer, stirring frequently, for about 5 minutes. Leave to go cold, then beat in the butter. Sandwich the two cakes together with about a third of the mixture, and use the remainder to cover the top and sides.

For the topping Press the toasted coconut over the surface of the gâteau. Cut the dates in half lengthways, remove the stones, then glaze the dates with honey. Arrange on top of the cake.

Carrot cake

In this Cranks variation of a traditional Swiss recipe the addition of carrots gives the cake a very moist texture

Carrots 6 oz (175 g)
Free-range eggs 2
Raw brown sugar 4 oz (100 g)
Oil 3 fl. oz (75 ml)
100% wholemeal self-raising flour 4 oz (100 g)
Ground cinnamon 1 tsp (5 ml)
Ground nutmeg ½ tsp (2.5 ml)
Desiccated coconut 2 oz (50 g)
Raisins 2 oz (50 g)

Orange icing
Butter or margarine 1½ oz (40 g)
Raw pale brown sugar 3 oz (75 g)
Orange, grated rind of ½
Shelled walnuts, chopped 1 oz (25 g)

Grease and line the base of a 7″ (18 cm) square cake tin. Finely grate the carrots. Whisk the eggs and sugar together until thick and creamy. Whisk in the oil slowly, then add the remaining ingredients and mix together to combine evenly. Spoon the mixture into the prepared tin. Level the surface and bake in the oven at 190°C (375°F/Mark 5) for 20–25 minutes, until firm to the touch and golden brown. Cool on a wire tray. Spread with orange icing when cold.

For the icing Beat the butter until soft, beat in the sugar and orange rind. Spread over the cake and sprinkle with chopped walnuts.

Honey cake

Clear honey ⅓ pt (200 ml)
Butter or margarine 1 oz (25 g)
100% wholemeal flour 6 oz (175 g)
Salt, pinch
Mixed spice ½ tsp (2.5 ml)
Ground nutmeg ¼ tsp (1.25 ml)
Ground cinnamon ¼ tsp (1.25 ml)
Free-range egg 1
Bicarbonate of soda ¾ tsp (3.75 ml)
Milk 3 tbsp (45 ml)
Flaked almonds 3 tbsp (45 ml)

Heat the honey and butter together until the butter has melted. Off the heat, beat in the flour, salt, spices and egg. Blend the bicarbonate of soda and milk together and stir into the mixture. Turn the mixture into a 9″ (23 cm) greased sandwich tin. Sprinkle the surface with flaked almonds and bake in the oven at 180°C (350°F/Mark 4) for 25–30 minutes, until golden and firm to the touch. Cool slightly before turning out on to a wire tray.

Poppyseed cake

Poppyseeds are usually thought of only as a decoration in baking, but this recipe proves their worth as a main ingredient

Poppyseeds 3 oz (75 g)
Milk ⅓ pt (190 ml)
Free-range eggs 2
Raw brown sugar 4 oz (100 g)
Oil ¼ pt (150 ml)
Almond essence 1 tsp (5 ml)
100% wholemeal self-raising flour 8 oz (225 g)

Skimmed milk powder 1½ oz (40 g)
Ground cinnamon 1 tsp (5 ml)

Grease and line the base of an 11 × 7″ (27 × 18 cm) cake tin. Soak 2 oz (50 g) poppyseeds in the milk for 1 hour. Whisk the eggs and sugar together until light and creamy. Very slowly whisk in the oil and almond essence until thoroughly mixed. Fold in the remaining ingredients. Pour the mixture into the prepared tin, sprinkle with remaining 1 oz (25 g) poppyseeds and bake in the oven at 190°C (375°F/Mark 5) for 20–25 minutes, until just firm to the touch. Cool on a wire tray. Cut into slices to serve.

Walnut sandwich cake

Butter or margarine 4 oz (100 g)
Raw brown sugar 4 oz (100 g)
Free-range eggs 2
100% wholemeal self-raising flour 5 oz (150 g)
Walnuts, chopped 2 oz (50 g)
Warm water 1 tbsp (15 ml)

Filling
Butter, softened 2 oz (50 g)
Raw brown sugar 2 oz (50 g)
Walnuts, chopped 2 tbsp (30 ml)

Grease and line the base of two 7″ (18 cm) sandwich tins. Cream the butter and sugar together until light and fluffy. Beat in the eggs, one at a time, then fold in the remaining ingredients. Divide the mixture between the prepared tins, level the surface and bake in the oven at 190°C (375°F/Mark 5) for 15–20 minutes, until risen and firm to the touch. Cool on a wire tray.

For the filling Cream the butter and sugar together until pale and fluffy. Stir in the walnuts. Use half the mixture and sandwich the two cakes together. Use the remaining filling to decorate the top of the cake.

Simnel cake

A special fruit cake originally made to celebrate Mothering Sunday, and now generally associated with Easter

Butter or margarine 8 oz (225 g)
Raw brown sugar 8 oz (225 g)
Free-range eggs 4
100% wholemeal flour 10 oz (300 g)
Salt, pinch
Currants 12 oz (350 g)
Sultanas 6 oz (175 g)
Lemon, grated rind of 1
Ground cinnamon 1 tsp (5 ml)
Ground nutmeg 1 tsp (5 ml)
Milk to mix
Mock marzipan (*see page 178*) 1½ lb (675 g)
Apricot jam

Grease and line an 8″ (20 cm) round cake tin. Cream the butter and sugar until pale and fluffy. Beat in the eggs one at a time. Combine the flour, salt, currants, sultanas, lemon rind and spices and fold into the creamed mixture. Add sufficient milk to give a 'dropping' consistency. Spoon half of the cake mixture into the prepared tin. Level the surface. Roll out one third of the marzipan to an 8″ (20 cm) round. Place on top of the cake mixture. Top with the remaining cake mixture and level the surface. Bake in the oven at 150°C (300°F/Mark 2) for about 2½ hours, or until firm to the touch. Cool in the tin.

The next day roll out half of the remaining marzipan to an 8″ (20 cm) round. Brush with apricot jam and press on to the top of the cake. Flute the edges and, with a knife, mark a lattice effect on the top. Use the remaining paste to make 11 balls. Position these on the edge of the cake using a little apricot jam.

Orange cake

Butter or margarine 4 oz (100 g)
Raw pale brown sugar 4 oz (100 g)

Small orange, grated rind & juice of 1
100% wholemeal self-raising flour 4 oz (100 g)
Salt, pinch
Water 1 tbsp (15 ml)
Free-range eggs, separated 2

Icing
Butter or margarine 2 oz (50 g)
Raw pale brown sugar 3 oz (75 g)
Small orange, grated rind & juice of 1
Walnuts, chopped, to decorate

Grease and line the base of two 7″ (18 cm) sandwich tins.
Cream the butter and sugar until light and fluffy. Beat in the
orange rind and juice and egg yolks. Fold in the flour and salt.
Whisk the egg whites until stiff and fold into the cake mixture.
Divide the mixture between the prepared tins. Level the
surface. Bake in the oven at 180°C (350°F/Mark 4) for about
15 minutes, until risen and just firm to the touch. Cool on a
wire tray.

For the icing Cream the butter and sugar until really pale and
fluffy. Beat in the orange rind and juice. Use half the icing to
sandwich the cakes together. Spread the remaining icing over
the top of the cake. Decorate the edge with chopped walnuts.

Date & walnut loaf

*The combination of date and walnut gives this cake a particularly
good flavour, especially if it's spread with butter*

Butter or margarine 5 oz (150 g)
Raw brown sugar 5 oz (150 g)
Free-range eggs, beaten 3
Small orange, grated rind & juice of 1
Stoned dates, chopped 5 oz (150 g)
Walnuts, chopped 3 oz (75 g)
100% wholemeal self-raising flour 10 oz (300 g)

Cream the butter and sugar together until pale and fluffy. Beat
in the eggs a little at a time. Stir in the orange rind. Fold in the

dates, 2 oz (50 g) walnuts and the flour, and lastly stir in the orange juice. Spoon the mixture into a greased and base-lined 2 lb (900 g) loaf tin. Level the surface, then sprinkle over the remaining chopped walnuts. Bake in the oven at 170°C (325°F/ Mark 3) for 1–1¼ hours, until risen and golden brown.

Orange gingercake

Gingercake is often considered to be one of the most difficult cakes to make, so follow this recipe carefully to ensure good results

100% wholemeal flour 8 oz (225 g)
Ground ginger 1½ tsp (7.5 ml)
Baking powder 1½ tsp (7.5 ml)
Bicarbonate of soda ½ tsp (2.5 ml)
Salt ½ tsp (2.5 ml)
Raw brown sugar 8 oz (225 g)
Black treacle 2 tbsp (30 ml)
Butter or margarine 3 oz (75 g)
Milk 4 tbsp (60 ml)
Free-range egg 1
Small orange, grated rind of 1
Orange juice 2 tbsp (30 ml)

Grease and line the base of an 11 × 7″ (27 × 18 cm) shallow cake tin. Put the first 5 ingredients in a mixing bowl. Heat together the sugar, treacle and butter until the butter is melted. Combine all the ingredients together, beat well and pour into the prepared tin. Bake in the oven at 170°C (325°F/ Mark 3) for about ½ hour, until just firm to the touch. Cool in the tin, then cut into squares.

Fruit cake without eggs (vegan)

This fruit cake, which was created for vegans, does not contain butter, eggs or milk and therefore has more limited keeping qualities

Mixed sultanas, currants & raisins 1½ lb (675 g)
Water ¾ pt (450 ml)
Oil ¼ pt (150 ml)

100% wholemeal self-raising flour 12 oz (350 g)
Blanched almonds, chopped 2 oz (50 g)
Molasses 1 tbsp (15 ml)
Lemon, grated rind of 1
Ground mixed spice 2 tsp (10 ml)
Raw brown sugar 3 oz (75 g)
Sherry or rum (optional) 3 tbsp (45 ml)

Grease and line a 7½″ (19 cm) round cake tin. Place all the ingredients, except the sherry, in a basin and beat well until evenly mixed. Pour into the prepared tin and bake in the oven at 150°C (300°F/Mark 2) for about 2 hours, until risen and firm to the touch. Allow to cool slightly in the tin, then spoon the sherry over the cake and leave in the tin until completely cold.

Unlike a traditional fruit cake, this cake does not keep for very long.

Barabrith

Based on the traditional Welsh recipe, this is similar to a teabread and should always be served buttered

Mixed dried fruit 10 oz (300 g)
Raw brown sugar 3 oz (75 g)
Lemon, grated rind of ½
Hot tea ⅔ pt (400 ml)
100% wholemeal flour 12 oz (350 g)
Baking powder 2 tsp (10 ml)
Mixed spice 2 tsp (10 ml)
Free-range egg 1

Put the fruit, sugar, lemon rind and tea in a basin. Cover and leave to soak overnight. Strain the fruit and reserve the liquid. Put the remaining ingredients into a mixing bowl, add the fruit and sufficient liquid to mix to a soft 'dropping' consistency – you may need to use all the liquid. Pour into a greased and base-lined 2 lb (900 g) loaf tin. Bake in the oven at 190°C (375°F/Mark 5) for 45–50 minutes, until risen and firm to the touch. Cool on a wire tray. Serve sliced and buttered.

Makes 1 large loaf

Wholemeal muffins

These light textured cakes, which are best served warm from the oven, are ideal for breakfast or with morning coffee

100% wholemeal flour 8 oz (225 g)
Barley flour 8 oz (225 g)
Baking powder 1 tsp (5 ml)
Salt ½ tsp (2.5 ml)
Raw brown sugar 4 oz (100 g)
Butter or margarine 1 oz (25 g)
Sultanas 4 oz (100 g)
Milk ½ pt (284 ml)
Honey or black treacle 2 tbsp (30 ml)
Bicarbonate of soda 1 tsp (5 ml)

Grease 18 patty tins. In a basin combine the flours, baking powder, salt and sugar. Rub in the butter and add the sultanas. Warm the milk and honey together until the honey is dissolved. Stir in the bicarbonate of soda and stir the liquid into the dry ingredients, beating well. Spoon the mixture into the tins and bake in the oven at 200°C (400°F/Mark 6) for 15–20 minutes, until risen and firm to the touch. Serve warm, with butter.

Makes 18 muffins

Bran muffins

100% wholemeal flour 14 oz (400 g)
Bran 2 oz (50 g)
Baking powder 1 tsp (5 ml)
Salt ½ tsp (2.5 ml)
Raw brown sugar 4 oz (100 g)
Butter or margarine 1 oz (25 g)
Milk ½ pt (284 ml)
Honey or black treacle 2 tbsp (30 ml)
Bicarbonate of soda 1 tsp (5 ml)

Grease 18 patty tins. In a basin combine the flour, bran, baking powder, salt and sugar. Rub in the butter or margar-

ine. Heat the milk and honey together then add to the dry
ingredients with the bicarbonate of soda. Beat well. Spoon the
mixture into the prepared tins and bake in the oven at 200°C
(400°F/Mark 6) for 15–20 minutes, until risen and firm to the
touch. Serve warm.

Makes 18 muffins

Apple buns

Rich, unusual and quickly made buns

Medium-sized cooking apples 2
100% wholemeal flour 8 oz (225 g)
Salt, pinch
Ground cinnamon ½ tsp (2.5 ml)
Baking powder 1 tsp (5 ml)
Butter or margarine 6 oz (175 g)
Raw brown sugar 2 oz (50 g)
Free-range egg, beaten 1

Core and dice the apples. Combine the flour, salt, spice and
baking powder in a basin. Rub in the butter until the mixture
resembles fine crumbs, then add the remaining ingredients
and combine well together. Place heaped spoonfuls on to a
lightly greased baking sheet and bake in the oven at 190°C
(375°F/Mark 5) for 20–25 minutes, until golden. Cool slightly
before transferring to a wire tray.

Makes 12 buns

Old English rock buns

*The term 'rock' suggests the appearance and not the texture of these
small cakes!*

100% wholemeal self-raising flour 8 oz (225 g)
Salt, pinch
Mixed spice 1 tsp (5 ml)
Butter or margarine 4 oz (100 g)
Raw Barbados sugar 3 oz (75 g)

Currants 2 oz (50 g)
Free-range egg 1
Milk 2 tbsp (30 ml)
Lemon, grated rind of ½

Combine the flour, salt and spice in a basin. Rub the fat into the flour, and then mix in the sugar and fruit. Beat the egg and add to the mixture, stir well. Add the milk and stir to give a soft but firm dough. Form into 'rocky' shapes and place on a greased baking sheet. Bake in the oven at 190°C (375°F/Mark 5) for about 15 minutes until just brown. Cool slightly on the baking sheet before transferring to a wire tray. Store in an airtight tin.

Makes about 8 buns

Raspberry buns

100% wholemeal self-raising flour 12 oz (350 g)
Ground nutmeg ½ tsp (2.5 ml)
Butter or margarine 4 oz (100 g)
Raw brown sugar 4 oz (100 g)
Currants 2 oz (50 g)
Free-range egg 1
Milk 2–3 tbsp (30–45 ml)
Raspberry jam 4 tbsp (60 ml)

Put flour and nutmeg in a basin, rub in the butter until the mixture resembles fine crumbs. Stir in the sugar and the currants. Beat the egg and add to the dry ingredients with sufficient milk to give a firm dough. Roll the dough into 12 balls. Place on a lightly greased baking sheet. Press a 'well' in the centre of each bun and fill with jam. Bake in the oven at 190°C (375°F/Mark 5) for about 20 minutes, until firm and golden. Cool on a wire tray.

Makes 12 buns

Walnut bars

Soft and chewy textured pieces of cake with roughly chopped walnuts added – quite delicious!

Oil 3 tbsp (45 ml)
Black treacle 1 tbsp (15 ml)
Raw brown sugar 4 oz (100 g)
Shelled walnuts, chopped 4 oz (100 g)
Free-range eggs 2
Vanilla essence 2 tsp (10 ml)
Wheatgerm 4 oz (100 g)
Salt ¼ tsp (1.25 ml)
Skimmed milk powder 2 oz (50 g)
Baking powder ½ tsp (2.5 ml)

Beat together the first 8 ingredients, then sift in the milk powder and baking powder. Beat well, then pour into a greased and base-lined 8″ (20 cm) square shallow cake tin. Bake in the oven at 180°C (350°F/Mark 4) for 25–30 minutes, until just firm to the touch. Cut into 'bars' while still warm.

Makes about 16 bars

'Chocolate' éclairs

Choux pastry (*see page 231*) 1 quantity
Fresh double cream ¼ pt (142 ml)

Carob icing
Carob bar 2.8 oz (80 g)
Butter or margarine 1 oz (25 g)

Lightly grease 2 baking sheets. Using a piping bag fitted with a ½″ (1 cm) plain nozzle, pipe choux pastry into 2½″ (6.5 cm) lengths. (If you do not have a piping bag, it is possible to spoon the choux pastry on to the baking sheets and although this does not give as 'professional' a finish, the result is perfectly acceptable.) Bake in the oven at 220°C (425°F/Mark 7) for 20–25 minutes, until risen and golden brown. They should be hollow and fairly dry. Make a slit in the side of each éclair with the tip of a knife. Cool on a wire tray.

For the icing Melt the carob bar and butter together over gentle heat. Whip the cream until it holds its shape and use to fill the éclairs, then dip in the carob icing, drawing each one across the surface of the icing and lifting to release it. Leave to set.

Makes about 12 éclairs

Fruit scones

Fruit scones are baked every morning in Cranks bakeries and are extremely popular with our customers at coffee time and with clotted cream teas in Cranks Dartington restaurant

100% wholemeal self-raising flour 8 oz (225 g)
Salt, pinch
Butter or margarine 3 oz (75 g)
Raw brown sugar 1 oz (25 g)
Sultanas 3 oz (75 g)
Milk, about 4 fl. oz (100 ml)

Put the flour and salt in a bowl. Rub in the butter until the mixture resembles fine crumbs. Stir in the sugar and sultanas, then add sufficient milk to give a soft, manageable dough. Knead gently on a lightly floured surface, then roll out about ¾″ (2 cm) thick. Stamp out 3″ (7.5 cm) rounds and roll to make the remaining scones. Place fairly close together on a lightly greased baking sheet and bake in the oven at 220°C (425°F/Mark 7) for 10–15 minutes, until golden. Cool on a wire tray. Best eaten on the day of making.

Makes 8 scones

Drop scones

Sometimes known as Scottish griddle scones, these are made from a rich batter which is dropped in spoonfuls on to a hot greased griddle to cook. Serve straight from the griddle with butter or honey

100% wholemeal self-raising flour 4 oz (100 g)
Sugar 1 oz (25 g)
Free-range egg 1
Milk, about 4 fl. oz (100 ml)

Beat all the ingredients together in a mixing bowl to give a fairly thick pouring consistency. Heat a griddle or frying pan to medium heat, brush lightly with oil or melted butter and drop spoonfuls of the mixture on to the griddle. Leave until bubbles appear on the surface and a 'skin' starts to form. Turn with a palette knife and cook until golden brown on the second side.

Makes about 12 scones

Cheese scones

Traditionally Cranks cheese scones are clover-shaped, and that's how you will see them in all the Cranks shops. At home a fluted round cutter would do well

100% wholemeal flour 1 lb (450 g)
Baking powder 2 tbsp (30 ml)
Salt, large pinch
Cayenne, large pinch
Butter or margarine 2 oz (50 g)
Cheddar cheese, grated 10 oz (300 g)
Milk, about ½ pt (284 ml)

Put the flour, baking powder, salt and cayenne in a basin. Rub in the butter until the mixture resembles fine crumbs. Stir in 8 oz (225 g) cheese and sufficient milk to give a soft, manageable dough. Knead gently, then roll out to 1" (2.5 cm) thickness. Stamp out 3" (7.5 cm) rounds with a fluted cutter. Brush with milk and sprinkle with the remaining cheese. Bake in the oven at 200°C (400°F/Mark 6) for about 20 minutes until golden. Cool on a wire tray.

Makes 15 scones

Brown sugar meringues

Meringues are popular with all ages, and using raw brown sugar gives them a particularly good taste. Sandwiched together with cream they are ideal for tea or as a dessert. It is advisable to sieve or mill the sugar before using it to remove any lumps

Egg whites 6
Salt, pinch
Raw pale brown sugar 12 oz (350 g)
Fresh double cream ½ pt (284 ml)

Stiffly whisk the egg whites with the salt until they stand in
'peaks'. Gradually whisk in the sugar a spoonful at a time until
the mixture is stiff again. Drop spoonfuls of the mixture on to
baking sheets lined with non-stick paper. If wished, you can
pipe shapes with a piping bag fitted with a star nozzle. Bake in
the oven at 120°C (250°F/Mark ½–1) for 3–4 hours, until
completely dried out and crisp. Just before serving, whip the
cream and use to sandwich the meringues together.

Makes about 20 meringues

Welsh butter cakes

*These are an extremely rich form of griddle scone. Handle with
care when cooking as the dough is delicate*

100% wholemeal flour 9 oz (275 g)
Baking powder ½ tsp (2.5 ml)
Ground nutmeg ½ tsp (2.5 ml)
Butter or margarine 6 oz (175 g)
Raw brown sugar 3 oz (75 g)
Currants 3 oz (75 g)
Free-range egg 1

Put the flour in a mixing bowl with the baking powder and
nutmeg. Rub in the butter, then add the remaining ingredients and work the mixture together to give soft manageable
dough. Roll out about ½″ (1.5 cm) thick on a lightly floured
board. Stamp out 3″ (7.5 cm) rounds. Lightly butter a griddle
or frying pan and cook the cakes on both sides over a medium
heat for about 5 minutes until golden. Serve warm.

Makes about 10 cakes

Coconut castles

Egg whites 2
Raw brown sugar 4 oz (100 g)
Desiccated coconut 6 oz (175 g)
Almond essence ½ tsp (2.5 ml)

Whisk the egg whites and sugar together until just frothy. Stir in the coconut and almond essence and shape the mixture into 8 'castles'. Place on a greased baking sheet and bake in the oven at 170°C (325°F/Mark 3) for about 35 minutes, until golden. Cool on a wire tray.

Makes 8 'castles'

Honey buns

An unusual recipe with an interesting result. These honey buns are deliciously sticky. Try serving them warm with vanilla ice-cream

Oil 6 fl. oz (170 ml)
Raw brown sugar 3 oz (75 g)
Fresh orange juice ¼ pt (150 ml)
100% wholemeal flour 1 lb (450 g)
Baking powder 2 tsp (10 ml)
Lemon, grated rind of ½
Shelled walnuts, roughly chopped 2 oz (50 g)

Syrup
Clear honey 4 fl. oz (100 ml)
Water 4 fl. oz (100 ml)
Raw brown sugar 4 oz (100 g)

Place oil, sugar, orange juice, flour, baking powder and lemon rind in a basin. Work together to give a soft dough. Shape into 12 ovals and press each one into the chopped walnuts. Place walnut-side up on a greased baking sheet. Bake in the oven at 190°C (370°F/Mark 5) for about 20 minutes, until golden and just firm to the touch. Meanwhile, put the ingredients for the syrup into a saucepan. Place over a gentle heat, stirring occasionally, until the sugar is dissolved. Bring to the boil and boil for 5 minutes. Spoon the mixture over the buns on the baking sheet and leave them to soak for 15 minutes, or until the syrup is absorbed. Cool on a wire tray covered with greaseproof paper.

Makes 12 buns

Truffle triangle

This lovely no-cook cake has a flavour that can be varied with the type of cake used to make the crumb base

Left-over cake 1½ lb (675 g)
Raw sugar mincemeat or apricot jam 4 oz (100 g)
Shelled walnuts, chopped 2 oz (50 g)
Carob powder 2 oz (50 g)
*Orange juice, sherry or rum 3–4 tbsp (45–60 ml)
Flaked almonds, toasted 4 tbsp (60 ml) to decorate

Carob Icing
Fresh double cream 5 tbsp (75 ml)
Carob bar 2.8 oz (80 g)

Crumble the cake into a basin, add the mincemeat, walnuts and carob powder and sufficient liquid to give a moist, yet firm consistency. Work the mixture together until fairly smooth. Turn the mixture on to a working surface and press into a triangular log shape. Place the cake on a wire tray with a baking sheet underneath.

For the icing Bring the cream to the boil, reduce heat. Break the carob bar into pieces and add to the cream. Stir over gentle heat until completely melted and smooth.

Carefully spoon the icing over the truffle triangle. Collect the icing that has run on to the tray, warm it gently and repeat the coating process. Sprinkle the flaked almonds on top and leave to set. Serve cut in slices.

---

* The quantity of liquid will vary with the type of cake crumbs used – add sufficient to give a moist yet firm consistency.

Biscuits

There are few products which so clearly illuminate the difference between wholemeal and bleached white flour as biscuits. Who could possibly opt for the flaccid white offering when presented with the option of the wholemeal biscuit with its warmth of colour, textural character and, of course, the incomparable nutty flavour of the 'real' food product?

One has to be honest and admit that a biscuit is really an unnecessary food, perhaps the ultimate 'snack', but we should not be too purist and we can admit the pleasure of the addition of a crisp tasty biscuit to the equally unnecessary but pleasurable social pause for a cup of coffee or tea.

In Cranks we store the biscuits appropriately in metal biscuit tins where they keep fresh for several days, but a sealed plastic bag is almost as good, provided the biscuits have been thoroughly cooled first.

Cranks flapjack

Butter or margarine 5 oz (150 g)
Raw brown sugar 3 oz (75 g)
Black treacle or black molasses 3 oz (75 g)
Porridge oats 8 oz (225 g)
Salt, pinch

Melt the butter, sugar and treacle in a pan – do not let it boil. Mix in the oats and salt and stir thoroughly. Press into an 8″ (20 cm) square tin and smooth over the surface with a palette knife. Bake in the oven at 190°C (375°F/Mark 5) for 25–30 minutes, until set and golden brown. Mark into portions while still warm, then leave to cool on a wire tray. Store in an airtight tin.

Makes 12 pieces

Melting moments

So called because they melt in the mouth

Butter or margarine 5 oz (150 g)
Raw brown sugar 3 oz (75 g)

Beaten egg 1 tbsp (15 ml)
Vanilla essence ½ tsp (2.5 ml)
100% wholemeal self-raising flour 4 oz (100 g)
Porridge oats, rolled 1 oz (25 g)
Extra porridge oats to coat

Cream the butter and sugar until light and fluffy. Beat in the egg and vanilla essence. Work in the flour and rolled oats. Form the mixture into balls the size of a walnut, and coat with rolled oats. Place well apart on a greased baking sheet and flatten slightly. Bake in the oven at 180°C (350°F/Mark 4) for 15–20 minutes, until golden. Cool slightly before transferring to a wire tray.

Makes 12–14 biscuits

Eccles cakes

Wholemeal shortcrust pastry (*see page 230*) 14 oz (400 g)
Currants 4 oz (100 g)
Lemon, coarsely grated rind of 1
Orange, coarsely grated rind of 1
Ground allspice ½ tsp (2.5 ml)
Ground nutmeg ½ tsp (2.5 ml)
Raw brown sugar 2 oz (50 g)
Butter or margarine 1 oz (25 g)
Egg white 1
Raw brown sugar to decorate

Roll out the pastry and use to stamp out ten 4" (10 cm) rounds. Mix together the currants, orange and lemon rind and spices. Melt the sugar and butter together and stir in the fruit. Cool. Put a spoonful of the mixture in the centre of each piece of pastry. Bring the edges together over the filling and seal them firmly by pinching together. Turn them over and press lightly to flatten. Place on a lightly greased baking sheet. Make a lattice pattern with a knife on top of each cake. Brush with beaten egg white and sprinkle with sugar. Bake in the oven at 220°C (425°F/Mark 7) for 15 minutes. Cool on a wire tray.

Makes 10 cakes

Date slices

Cooked stoned dates sandwiched between an oaty mixture and baked until golden

Dates (or dried apricots or figs) chopped 12 oz (350 g)
Water 6 tbsp (90 ml)
Lemon, grated rind of ½
100% wholemeal flour 8 oz (225 g)
Porridge oats 4 oz (100 g)
Raw brown sugar 3 oz (75 g)
Butter or margarine, melted 5 oz (150 g)

Put the dates, water and lemon rind in a saucepan. Heat gently, stirring occasionally until the mixture is soft. Combine the remaining ingredients and sprinkle half the mixture into an 11 × 7″ (27 × 18 cm) shallow cake tin and press down well. Cover with the dates and sprinkle the remaining oat mixture over and press down firmly. Bake in the oven at 200°C (400°F/Mark 6) for 20 minutes. Cool in the tin and then cut into slices.

Makes 16 slices

Carob crunch

A rich, crunchy biscuit which has been made in Cranks for over twenty years

Butter or margarine, melted 4 oz (100 g)
Carob powder 2 tsp (10 ml)
100% wholemeal flour 4 oz (100 g)
Baking powder 1 tsp (5 ml)
Raw brown sugar 2½ oz (65 g)
Desiccated coconut 2 oz (50 g)

Melt the butter in a saucepan and stir in the carob powder. Add the remaining ingredients and mix together. Press the mixture into a 7″ (18 cm) sandwich tin and smooth over with a palette knife. Bake in the oven at 190°C (375°F/Mark 5) for 25 minutes, until just set and golden. Mark into wedges while still hot, and allow to cool before taking out of the tin.

For special occasions, cover with CAROB ICING (*see page 196*).

Makes 8 biscuits

Shortbread

Butter or margarine 4 oz (100 g)
100% wholemeal flour 6 oz (175 g)
Raw brown sugar 2 oz (50 g)

Cut the butter into the flour with a palette knife and rub in until the mixture resembles breadcrumbs, then add the sugar. Work the mixture together to give a firm dough. Press into a 7″ (18 cm) round tin, neaten the edges with a fork and use the prongs to make a decorative pattern. Mark into 8 portions and bake in the oven at 150°C (300°F/Mark 2) for about 45 minutes. Cut into pieces while warm, but leave to cool in the tin.

The same mixture can be used for making individual biscuits.

For special occasions coat with CAROB ICING (*see page 196*)

Makes 8 pieces

Country biscuits

Classic biscuits with a wholesome nutty texture, so versatile that they can be served with sweet or savoury foods

100% wholemeal flour 6 oz (175 g)
Coarse oatmeal 1½ oz (40 g)
Baking powder 1 tsp (5 ml)
Salt ½ tsp (2.5 ml)
Butter or margarine 3 oz (75 g)
Raw brown sugar 2 oz (50 g)
Milk (or soya milk) to mix 3 tbsp (45 ml)

Mix all the dry ingredients, except the sugar, together. Rub in the butter until the mixture resembles fine crumbs, stir in the sugar and add milk. Stir well until the dough is firm but manageable. Roll out fairly thinly on a lightly floured board and stamp out 3″ (7.5 cm) rounds. Place on a greased baking sheet and bake in the oven at 180°C (350°F/Mark 4) for 20–25 minutes, until light brown. Cool on a wire tray and store in an airtight tin.

Try sandwiching the biscuits together with jam in the middle – ideal for children.

Makes about 18 biscuits

Coconut biscuits

Butter or margarine 4 oz (100 g)
100% wholemeal self-raising flour 4 oz (100 g)
Raw brown sugar 4 oz (100 g)
Desiccated coconut 4 oz (100 g)
Salt, pinch
Free-range egg 1

Rub the butter into the flour until the mixture resembles fine crumbs, then stir in the sugar, coconut and salt. Mix well, stir in the egg, then mix to a soft dough. Roll out fairly thinly on a lightly floured board and stamp into 3″ (7.5 cm) rounds. Place on a greased baking sheet. Bake in the oven at 180°C (350°F/Mark 4) for about 15 minutes, or until golden brown. Cool on a wire tray and store in an airtight tin.

Makes about 20 biscuits

Carob chip cookies

A wholefood version of American chocolate chip cookies

Butter or margarine 6 oz (175 g)
100% wholemeal self-raising flour 8 oz (225 g)
Raw brown sugar 4 oz (100 g)
Salt, pinch
Free-range egg 1
Carob bar, chopped 2.8 oz (80 g)

Rub the butter into the flour until the mixture resembles fine crumbs. Add the sugar, salt and egg and mix well. Stir in the carob 'chips' and mix to a soft dough. Chill the dough for ½ hour, then roll out on a lightly floured surface to ¼" (6 mm) thickness. Stamp out 3½" (9 cm) rounds and place well apart on lightly greased baking sheets. Mark with the prongs of a fork. Bake in the oven at 180°C (350°F/Mark 4) for 10–12 minutes, until golden. Cool slightly, then transfer to a wire tray.

Makes 15 cookies

Florentines

These are easy to prepare, but care must be taken when cooling, removing from the non-stick paper and storing as these biscuits are delicate

Butter or margarine 3 oz (75 g)
Raw brown sugar 4 oz (100 g)
Shelled walnuts, chopped 4 oz (100 g)
Flaked almonds 2 oz (50 g)
Dried fruit, e.g. stoned dates, raisins, chopped 2 oz (50 g)
100% wholemeal flour 1 tbsp (15 ml)

Melt the butter and sugar together in a saucepan over gentle heat. Add the remaining ingredients. Line baking sheets with non-stick paper and drop large spoonfuls of the mixture well apart on the prepared sheets. Press into neat shapes. Bake in the oven at 180°C (350°F/Mark 4) for 12–15 minutes, until golden. Leave until cold before removing from the paper.

Makes 12 biscuits

Sesame thins

Baked sesame seeds give these crisp, golden biscuits a unique flavour

100% wholemeal flour 4 oz (100 g)
Butter or margarine 4 oz (100 g)

Sesame seeds 2 oz (50 g)
Pale raw brown sugar 2 oz (50 g)

Put the flour in a basin, rub in the butter. Add the sesame seeds and sugar and work the mixture together. Press the mixture into an 11 × 7″ (27 × 18 cm) shallow cake tin. Bake in the oven at 180°C (350°F/Mark 4) for about 20 minutes, until golden. Mark into slices while warm but leave to cool in the tin.

Makes 12 biscuits

Millet & peanut cookies

A recipe specially devised for this book, but since their introduction into Cranks shops these cookies have become a great favourite

Oil 4 tbsp (60 ml)
Salt ¼ tsp (1.25 ml)
Free-range egg 1
Raw brown sugar 3 oz (75 g)
Peanuts, ground 4 oz (100 g)
Raisins 3 oz (75 g)
Millet flakes 4 oz (100 g)

Lightly whisk together the oil, salt, egg and sugar. Stir in the remaining ingredients until well blended. Roll the mixture into 10 balls. Place on a lightly greased baking sheet. Press each one down to flatten slightly. Bake in the oven at 180°C (350°F/Mark 4) for about 15 minutes, until golden. Allow to cool on the baking sheet for a few minutes before transferring to a wire tray.

Makes 10 cookies

Caraway bran biscuits

An old-fashioned recipe with a distinctive flavour

Butter or margarine 2 oz (50 g)
Raw brown sugar 2 oz (50 g)
100% wholemeal self-raising flour 4 oz (100 g)

Bran ½ oz (15 g)
Caraway seeds 1 tbsp (15 ml)
Free-range egg 1

Cream the butter and sugar together until light and fluffy.
Add the flour, bran, caraway seeds and egg and work together
to form a soft dough. Roll out fairly thinly on a lightly floured
surface and stamp out 3″ (7.5 cm) rounds. Place on a greased
baking sheet and bake in the oven at 180°C (350°F/Mark 4) for
10–15 minutes, until golden. Cool on a wire tray and store in
an airtight tin.

Makes about 18 biscuits

Crunchies

Butter or margarine 4 oz (100 g)
Raw brown sugar 4 oz (100 g)
100% wholemeal self-raising flour 6 oz (175 g)
Crunchy breakfast cereal 2 oz (50 g)
Currants 1 oz (25 g)
Molasses 1 tbsp (15 ml)
Mixed spice ½ tsp (2.5 ml)

Melt the butter in a saucepan. Off the heat, stir in all the
remaining ingredients until evenly blended. Press the mixture
into 10 even-sized balls and place well apart on a lightly
greased baking sheet. Bake in the oven at 180°C (350°F/Mark
4) for 12–15 minutes. Allow to cool slightly on the baking
sheet before transferring to a wire tray.

Makes 10 biscuits

Peanut rounds

Butter or margarine 4 oz (100 g)
Raw brown sugar 4 oz (100 g)
Free-range egg 1
Peanut butter 3 oz (75 g)
Peanuts, roughly chopped 3 oz (75 g)
100% wholemeal flour 3 oz (75 g)

Baking powder ½ tsp (2.5 ml)
Flaked wheat 5 oz (150 g)

Cream the butter and sugar together until light and fluffy. Beat in the egg, then add the remaining ingredients and work the mixture together to give a manageable dough. Roll out fairly thinly on a lightly floured surface and stamp out 3″ (7.5 cm) rounds with a fluted cutter. Place on a greased baking sheet and bake in the oven at 190°C (375°F/Mark 5) for about 15 minutes, until golden. Cool on a wire tray. Store in an airtight tin.

Makes about 25 biscuits

Gingernuts

Really dark crunchy biscuits

Butter or margarine 2½ oz (60 g)
100% wholemeal self-raising flour 6 oz (175 g)
Raw brown sugar 2½ oz (60 g)
Black treacle 4 oz (100 g)
Bicarbonate of soda ¾ tsp (3.75 ml)
Ground ginger 2 tsp (10 ml)

Rub the butter into the flour until the mixture resembles fine crumbs. Stir in the sugar. Warm the treacle in a saucepan, stir in the bicarbonate of soda and ginger. Add the ginger mixture to the dry ingredients, knead well to form a soft dough. Roll the mixture into balls about the size of a walnut. Place well apart on oiled baking sheets, flatten slightly. Bake in the oven at 180°C (350°F/Mark 4) for about 15 minutes. Allow to cool slightly on the baking sheets before transferring to a wire tray.

Makes about 15 biscuits

Cheesejacks

This is a savoury variation of Cranks flapjacks and is particularly popular with children

Porridge oats 5 oz (150 g)
Cheddar cheese, grated 6 oz (175 g)
Free-range egg, beaten 1
Butter or margarine, melted 2 oz (50 g)
Rosemary, crushed ½ tsp (2.5 ml)
Salt & pepper to taste

Combine all the ingredients together. Mix well. Then press into a shallow 7" (18 cm) square cake tin. Bake in the oven at 180°C (350°F/Mark 4) for about 40 minutes, until golden. Cut into slices. Serve hot or cold.

Makes 12 slices

Cheese biscuits

Mouthwatering savoury biscuits, ideal to serve with drinks

100% wholemeal flour 4 oz (100 g)
Butter, softened 4 oz (100 g)
Cheddar cheese, grated 4 oz (100 g)
Paprika, pinch

Work the ingredients together to give a soft, manageable dough. Roll out on a lightly floured surface to ⅛" (3 mm) thick and stamp out rounds or cut into straws. Bake in the oven at 200°C (400°F/Mark 6) for 5–8 minutes, depending on size. Cool on a wire rack.

Wholemeal rusks

These thin fingers of bread, flavoured with diluted yeast extract and baked until crisp, are particularly good for teething babies and young children

Day-old wholemeal bread
Yeast extract (such as Barmene or Yeastrel)

Cut the bread into ½" (1.5 cm) fingers. Dilute 1 teaspoon Barmene or Yeastrel stirred into ½ pt (300 ml) boiling water. Brush the sides and edges of the bread with the yeast extract and bake in the oven at 150°C (300°F/Mark 2) for about 1 hour, until really crisp and dried.

Melba toast

Day-old wholemeal bread

Cut the bread into wafer-thin slices with a sharp serrated knife. Arrange in a single layer on a baking sheet and bake in the oven at 200°C (400°F/Mark 6) for 7–8 minutes, until really crisp and golden. Cool on a wire tray, then keep in an airtight container.

Breakfast Cereals

It was as long ago as 1926 that Dr Bircher-Benner published a small book promoting the importance to health of the inclusion of a good proportion of raw food in the diet. One of the uncooked dishes he invented was 'Raw fruit porridge' or 'Muesli' and this became a standard stocked line in health food shops throughout Europe, and has recently appeared on the shelves of supermarkets in response to a growing public demand, although one suspects that the product now bears little relation to Dr Bircher-Benner's original intention. In any case, he stressed the importance of preparing the dish just before it is to be eaten. He believed that the nutritional value of the dish came from the interaction of all the materials united by nature within a single food. In terms of energy, he thought 'that this value resided in the calculated and graded play of rainbow colours inside the food, considered as a total combination of the energies of sunlight'.

There are, of course, breakfast cereals other than muesli, and it is not necessary to turn to packets of brand named products when these can so easily be made at home, and with all the 'right' ingredients. These home-made cereals can be put together in their dry condition, lightly toasted and stored in airtight tins for a number of weeks.

Breakfast cereal

Popular with all the family this delicious crunchy breakfast cereal is a 'full of goodness' way to start the day

Porridge oats 14 oz (400 g)
Sunflower seeds 2 oz (50 g)
Mixed nuts, chopped 4 oz (100 g)
Wheatgerm 4 oz (100 g)
Desiccated coconut 3 oz (75 g)
Sesame seeds 1 oz (25 g)
Raw brown sugar 4 oz (100 g)
Water ¼ pt (150 ml)
Oil ¼ pt (150 ml)
Vanilla essence ½ tsp (2.5 ml)
Salt ½ tsp (2.5 ml)

Combine the first 7 ingredients in a large mixing bowl. Whisk together the water, oil, vanilla and salt, then stir in the dry ingredients. Mix well. Spread the cereal over the base of a large, shallow roasting tin and bake in the oven at 190°C (375°F/Mark 5) for 20–30 minutes, turning occasionally until crisp and golden. Leave to cool. Store in an airtight container.

Makes 2¼ lb (1 kg)

Muesli

The Cranks version of the original Swiss recipe, so versatile that it can be served at any time – not just for breakfast

Porridge oats 4 oz (100 g)
Sultanas 2 tbsp (30 ml)
Fresh orange juice ½ pt (300 ml)
Eating apples, grated 2
Milk to mix
Chopped nuts
Honey

Put the oats, sultanas and orange juice in a mixing bowl. Cover and leave to soak overnight. Stir in the apple and sufficient milk to give a 'soft' consistency. Spoon the muesli into dishes and top with chopped nuts and honey.

Serves 4–6

Milled wholewheat berries & nuts

Wholewheat 4 oz (100 g)
Finely chopped nuts 4 tbsp (60 ml)
Honey to taste
Milk to taste

Pass the wheat through a wheat mill or grind in a coffee grinder. Mix with the nuts and serve with milk and honey as a breakfast cereal.

Serves 6

Bread

Bread seen as 'the staff of life' obviously played a much larger part in mankind's diet in the past than it does today. We would no doubt benefit greatly were we to return to a much simpler mode of living and eating, with bread in its proper central role as provider of health through its abundance of essential elements. Proteins, carbohydrates, vitamins, minerals and trace elements are all contained in a living relationship in the 100% wholemeal loaf. This is made from flour which has had nothing taken away and nothing added, but is just as nature intended!

All Cranks bread, and in fact all Cranks bakery products, are made with only the 100% wholemeal form of English, compost-grown stoneground flour. Our bread style, which is close and moist, was originally based on Doris Grant's recipe for a home-produced wholemeal loaf. Many of our recipes for other breads simply use the basic wholemeal dough and then modify it with the addition of other ingredients such as bran, cheese, eggs, molasses, etc.

Cranks wholemeal bread

This is the Cranks adaptation of Doris Grant's original recipe, which had been invented to help the busy housewife who wanted to make her own bread. It is somewhat unconventional in method as it eliminates kneading

For 2 large loaves
100% wholemeal flour 3 lbs (1.35 kg)
Sea salt 1 tbsp (15 ml)
Fresh yeast (if unobtainable, use dried yeast) 1 oz (25 g)
Barbados sugar 1 tbsp (15 ml)
Water 1½–2 pts (900 ml–1.2 l)

For 1 loaf or 6 baps
100% wholemeal flour 1 lb (450 g)
Sea salt 1 tsp (5 ml)
Fresh yeast ½ oz (15 g)
Barbados sugar 1 tsp (5 ml)
Water ½–⅔ pt (300–400 ml)

Mix flour with salt (in very cold weather warm the flour slightly, enough to take the chill off). Mix the yeast and sugar in a small bowl with ¼ pt (150 ml) of the warm water. Leave in a warm place for 10 minutes or so to froth up. Pour the yeasty liquid into the flour and gradually add the rest of the water. Mix well – by hand is best. Divide the dough into two 2 pt bread tins (round cake tins may be used if necessary) which have first been greased and warmed. Put the tins in a warm place, cover with a cloth or oiled polythene, and leave for about 20 minutes to rise, or until the dough is within ½" of the top of the tins. Bake in the oven at 200°C (400°F/Mark 6) for about 35–40 minutes. Allow to cool for a few minutes and turn out on to a wire tray.

For baps Roll out the dough thickly on a lightly floured surface and stamp out six 4" (100 cm) rounds. Place on a baking sheet, brush lightly with milk and leave in a warm place to prove for 10–15 minutes. Bake in the oven at 200°C (400°F/Mark 6) for 20–25 minutes. Cool on a wire tray. Split and butter – delicious filled with cottage cheese and lettuce.

Corn & molasses bread

100% wholemeal flour 8 oz (225 g)
Cornmeal 4 oz (100 g)
Salt ½ tsp (2.5 ml)
Butter, margarine or white fat 1 oz (25 g)
Fresh yeast ½ oz (15 g)
Raw brown sugar 1 tsp (5 ml)
Water, about ¼ pt (150 ml)
Molasses 1 tbsp (15 ml)

Put the flour, cornmeal and salt in a basin. Rub in the butter. Put the yeast and sugar in a small basin, stir in half the warm water and leave in a warm place for about 10 minutes, until frothy. Pour the yeast on to the flour, add the molasses and sufficient water to mix to a soft, but not sticky, dough. Knead gently on a lightly floured surface for 5 minutes, then place in a greased 1 lb (450 g) loaf tin. Make 3 deep cuts lengthwise across the top. Cover with oiled polythene and leave in a warm place until the bread reaches the top of the tin. Bake in the oven at 200°C (400°F/Mark 6) for 25–30 minutes. Remove from the tin and cool on a wire tray.

Makes 1 small loaf

Rye Bread

Rye bread is not particularly easy to make and practice may be necessary to achieve a good result. However, it is worthwhile to persevere as this bread is crusty on the outside yet soft textured with a distinctive flavour

100% wholemeal flour 1 lb (450 g)
Coarse rye meal (or flour) 6 oz (175 g)
Salt 1½ tsp (7.5 ml)
Caraway seeds 1½ tsp (7.5 ml)
Butter or margarine 2 oz (50 g)
Fresh yeast ¾ oz (20 g)
Raw brown sugar 1 tbsp (15 ml)
Water ½–⅔ pt (300–400 ml)

Glaze
Water 1 tsp (5 ml)
Raw brown sugar ½ tsp (2.5 ml)

Combine the flour, rye meal, salt and 1 tsp (5 ml) caraway seeds in a large mixing bowl. Rub the butter in until well blended. Mix together the yeast, sugar and ¼ pt (150 ml) warm water. Set aside in a warm place until frothy – about 10 minutes. Add the frothy liquid to the flour with ¼ pt (150 ml) water. Work to a soft dough by hand, adding extra water as necessary. Cover and leave for 5 minutes. Knead on a lightly floured surface and form the dough into a neat cob shape. Place on a lightly greased baking sheet. Combine the water and sugar for the glaze and brush over the top of the loaf. Sprinkle the remaining ½ tsp (2.5 ml) caraway seeds over. Make 3 long slashes in the top of the loaf. Cover with oiled polythene and leave in a warm place until doubled in size. Remove the polythene and bake in the oven at 200°C (400°F/Mark 6) for 40–50 minutes.

If the loaf sounds hollow when tapped on the base, it means it is cooked.

For a softer crust, place a tin of water in the bottom of the oven during cooking.

Makes 1 large loaf

Bran bread

A basic wholemeal bread dough with added roughage in the form of bran

100% wholemeal flour 1 lb (450 g)
Bran 3 oz (75 g)
Salt 1 tsp (5 ml)
Butter, margarine or white fat 1 oz (25 g)
Fresh yeast ½ oz (15 g)
Raw brown sugar 1 tbsp (15 ml)
Water, about ½ pt (300 ml)

Combine the flour, bran and salt in a large basin. Rub in the butter until well blended. Mix together the yeast, sugar, and half the warm water and leave in a warm place until frothy. Add the yeast mixture to the flour and mix together, adding sufficient warm water to give a soft, but not sticky, dough. Cover and leave to rest for 5 minutes. Knead on a lightly floured surface, then press into a greased 2 lb (900 g) loaf tin. Cut 2 slashes in the top. Cover with oiled polythene and leave in a warm place to rise until the mixture reaches the top of the tin. Bake in the oven at 200°C (400°F/Mark 6) for 40–50 minutes. Cool on a wire tray.

Makes 1 large loaf

Barley bread

Barley flour produces a light textured bread, pale in colour and unusual in flavour

*Barley flour 1 lb (450 g)
Salt 1 tsp (5 ml)
Fresh yeast ½ oz (15 g)
Raw brown sugar 1 tsp (5 ml)
Water, up to ½ pt (300 ml)

Follow the method for BRAN BREAD (*see previous recipe*).

Makes 1 large loaf

Soya bread

100% wholemeal flour 14 oz (400 g)
Soya flour 2 oz (50 g)
Salt 1 tsp (5 ml)
Raw brown sugar 1 tsp (5 ml)
Fresh yeast ½ oz (15 g)
Water, about ⅓ pt (200 ml)

Put the flours and the salt in a mixing bowl. Take 2 large spoonfuls of the flour and mix with the sugar, fresh yeast and half the warm water. Leave in a warm place for about 20 minutes, until frothy. Combine all the ingredients together and mix to a soft dough. On a lightly floured surface, knead the dough for a few minutes then shape and place in a greased 1 lb (450 g) loaf tin. Brush the top of the dough with oil, cover with oiled polythene and put in a warm place until the dough comes to the top of the tin. Bake in the oven at 200°C (400°F/ Mark 6) for 25–30 minutes. Cool on a wire tray.

Makes 1 small loaf

Sourdough bread

This unusual method of breadmaking produces a sharp-flavoured loaf

---

* We recommend Mrs Horsefield's barley flour, which is a finely balanced mix of barley and wheat.

Fresh yeast 1 tbsp (15 ml)
Water 1¾ pt (1 l)
Raw brown sugar 1 tsp (5 ml)
100% wholemeal flour 4 lb (1.8 kg)
Salt 1 tbsp (15 ml)
Oil 3 tbsp (45 ml)

Mix the yeast, ½ pt (300 ml) warm water, sugar and 8 oz (225 g) flour to a smooth paste. Cover and leave to 'sour' at room temperature for up to 5 days. Put 3 lb (1.4 kg) flour and remaining water into a large basin, stir in the 'soured starter' and mix well to a soft dough. Cover with a wet teatowel and leave in a warm place for 8 hours or overnight. Beat well, then stir in the remaining ingredients. Knead for 5 minutes on a lightly floured surface. Divide the mixture between three 2 lb (900 g) oiled loaf tins. Cover with oiled polythene and leave in a warm place to rise until doubled in size. Bake in the oven at 200°C (400°F/Mark 6) for 35–40 minutes. Cool on a wire tray.

Instead of making a fresh 'starter' each time, it is possible to reserve some of the dough in the refrigerator and to use this as the starter for more loaves as required.

Makes 3 loaves

Cheese bread

Free-range egg, beaten 1
Cheddar cheese, grated ½ lb (225 g)
Wholemeal bread dough, using 1 lb (450 g) flour (*see page 214*)

Work the egg and cheese into the dough. Place the dough in a lightly greased 2 lb (900 g) loaf tin. Continue as for CRANKS WHOLEMEAL BREAD (*see page 214*).

Makes 1 large loaf

Garlic bread

This is delicious served hot with soups and salads

Garlic cloves, crushed 3
Wholemeal bread dough, using 1 lb (450 g) flour (*see page 214*)

Knead the garlic into the dough. Continue as for CRANKS WHOLEMEAL BREAD (*see page 214*).

Makes 1 large loaf

Cheese baps

This is one of the most popular of all Cranks recipes. The baps can be served split, buttered and filled with mustard and cress

Free-range egg, beaten 1
Wholemeal bread dough, using 1 lb (450 g) flour (*see page 214*)
Cheddar cheese, grated 9 oz (275 g)

Work the egg into the dough until evenly mixed. Roll out the dough on a lightly floured surface to a rectangle 15 × 10" (39 × 25 cm). Sprinkle a third of the cheese over the centre third of the dough. Fold the left-hand third of the dough over the cheese. Sprinkle another third of the cheese over the double thickness of dough, then fold the right-hand side of the dough towards the centre to cover the cheese completely. Press down well. Stamp out 4" (10 cm) rounds, folding and rolling trimmings to make the last baps. Place on a floured baking sheet and brush lightly with milk. Sprinkle with the remaining cheese and leave in a warm place to prove for 10–15 minutes. Bake in the oven at 200°C (400°F/Mark 6) for about 25 minutes. Cool on a wire tray.

Makes 6 baps

Herb bread

An interesting variation of wholemeal bread which adds extra flavour to sandwiches

Wholemeal bread dough, using 1 lb (450 g) flour (*see page 214*)
Oregano 2 tsp (10 ml)
Rosemary 1½ tsp (7.5 ml)
Turmeric (optional) 1 tsp (5 ml)
Sage ½ tsp (2.5 ml)

Knead all the ingredients together until evenly distributed. Continue as for CRANKS WHOLEMEAL BREAD (*see page 214*).

Makes 1 large loaf

Granary cob

Granary bread has become so popular in the last few years because of its nutty flavour and texture

100% wholemeal flour 1 lb (450 g)
Rye flour 2 oz (50 g)
Cracked wheat 4 oz (100 g)
Salt 1 tsp (5 ml)
Fresh yeast ½ oz (15 g)
Sugar 1 tsp (5 ml)
Black treacle 1 oz (25 g)
Water, about ¾ pt (450 ml)
Cracked wheat, to sprinkle

Combine the flours, cracked wheat and salt. Continue as for CRANKS WHOLEMEAL BREAD (*see page 214*), adding the black treacle with the water. On a floured surface knead lightly and shape into 2 rounds. Place on greased baking sheets. Brush with water or milk and sprinkle with cracked wheat. Leave to rise in a warm place until doubled in size – about 45 minutes. Bake in the oven at 200°C (400°F/Mark 6) for about 30 minutes.

Makes 2 cobs

Four grain bread

Rye flour 4 oz (100 g)
Barley flour 4 oz (100 g)

100% wholemeal flour 4 oz (100 g)
Medium oatmeal 4 oz (100 g)
Salt 1 tsp (5 ml)
Fresh yeast ½ oz (15 g)
Raw brown sugar 1 tsp (5 ml)
Water, about ⅓ pt (200 ml)

Put the first 5 ingredients into a bowl. Take a few spoonfuls of the flour mixture and mix with the yeast, sugar and half the warm water. Leave in a warm place until frothy – about 20 minutes. Combine all the ingredients together, adding sufficient warm water to give a soft, manageable dough. Knead well on a lightly floured surface, then put into a 2 lb (900 g) oiled loaf tin. Cover and leave to rise until the mixture reaches the top of the tin. Bake in the oven at 200°C (400°F/Mark 6) for 35–40 minutes. Cool on a wire tray.

Makes 1 large loaf

Pumpernickel

An unusual bread that is steamed in a pudding basin rather than baked. Steaming and the absence of yeast produce a close textured loaf

* Rye flour 2 lb (900 g)
Salt 2 tsps (10 ml)
Hot water 1–1½ pt (600–900 ml)
Molasses 4 tbsp (60 ml)

Put the flour and salt in a basin. Mix the molasses with 1 pt (600 ml) water and add to the flour. Mix well, adding extra water if necessary to give a soft dough. Divide the mixture between 2 well-greased 6" (15 cm) pudding basins (the basins should be three-quarters full). Cover with buttered greaseproof paper or foil, with a pleat in it to allow for expansion. Place the basins in a pan of hot water. Cover and simmer for up to 5 hours. Refill the pan as necessary. Turn out and cool

* Other coarse flours may be used to vary the colour and flavour of the finished loaves.

on a wire tray. When cold, wrap in greaseproof paper and refrigerate. Serve thinly sliced.

Makes 2 loaves

Unyeasted bread

This dough will not rise like a traditional yeast dough, but is improved by standing before baking. The result is a crusty loaf with a close texture and good keeping qualities

100% wholemeal flour 1½ lb (675 g)
Salt 1½ tsp (7.5 ml)
Water ¾ pt (450 ml)

Combine the flour and salt in a mixing bowl and stir in sufficient warm water to mix to a soft dough. Knead for 5 minutes on a lightly floured surface, then return to the mixing bowl. Cover with a damp cloth and leave in a warm place overnight or up to 24 hours. Turn out on to a lightly floured surface and knead for a further 5 minutes. Place in an oiled 2 lb (900 g) loaf tin, cover and leave in a warm place for up to 4 hours. Bake in the oven at 200°C (400°F/Mark 6) for about ½ an hour, until easily removed from the tin. Cool on a wire tray.

Makes 1 large loaf

Oatmeal soda bread

This traditional Irish bread does not include yeast and therefore is best served on the day of making

100% wholemeal flour 1 lb (450 g)
Fine oatmeal 4 oz (100 g)
Cream of tartar 1½ tsp (7.5 ml)
Bicarbonate of soda 1 tsp (5 ml)
Salt ½ tsp (2.5 ml)
Butter or margarine 1 oz (25 g)
Mixed milk & water, about ¾ pt (450 ml)

Put the dry ingredients into a mixing bowl. Rub in the butter, then quickly stir in the milk and water to give a very soft consistency. Turn the mixture into a lightly greased 9″ (23 cm) sandwich tin and bake in the oven at 230°C (450°F/Mark 8) for 15 minutes. Reduce heat to 180°C (350°F/Mark 4) for a further 15–20 minutes, until golden. Cool on a wire tray.

Apple & banana bread

A sweet and moist fruit bread that can be sliced and buttered at tea time

Medium-sized apple 1
100% wholemeal flour 1 lb (450 g)
Yeast ½ oz (15 g)
Water ¼ pt (150 ml)
Raw brown sugar 2 oz (50 g)
Salt 1 tsp (5 ml)
Ground cinnamon 1 tsp (10 ml)
Ground nutmeg 1tsp (5 ml)
Sultanas 2 oz (50 g)
Small bananas, mashed 2
Lemon, grated rind of ½

Chop and steam the apple until tender. Press through a sieve to make a purée and leave to cool. Mix together 4 oz (100 g) flour, yeast and warm water until smooth, leave in a warm place until frothy. Combine the remaining flour, sugar, salt, spices and sultanas in a basin. Stir in the yeast mixture, apple purée, mashed banana and lemon and beat well. Divide the mixture between two greased 1 lb (450 g) loaf tins. Leave to prove in a warm place until the mixture reaches the top of the tin. Bake in the oven at 190°C (375°F/Mark 5) for about 35 minutes.

Makes 2 small loaves

Spiced currant bread

Wholemeal bread dough, using 1 lb (450 g) flour (*see page 214*)
Molasses 1 tbsp (15 ml)
Free-range egg, beaten 1

Currants 4 oz (100 g)
Mixed spice 2 tsp (10 ml)
Clear honey to glaze

Work all the ingredients together until well blended. Place the dough in a lightly greased 2 lb (900 g) loaf tin. Continue as for CRANKS WHOLEMEAL BREAD (*see page 214*). Brush the top with honey while still warm.

Makes 1 large loaf

Walnut tea bread

100% wholemeal flour 10 oz (300 g)
Porridge oats 2 oz (50 g)
Wheatgerm ½ oz (15 g)
Salt 1 tsp (5 ml)
Walnuts, chopped 2 oz (50 g)
Fresh yeast ½ oz (15 g)
Raw brown sugar 2 tsp (10 ml)
Water ¼–⅓ pt (150–200 ml)
Honey 2 tbsp (30 ml)
Oil 2 tbsp (30 ml)

In a mixing bowl combine the flour, oats, wheatgerm, salt and walnuts. Mix together the yeast, sugar and half the warm water. Leave in a warm place until frothy. Add to the mixture together with the honey, oil and sufficient warm water to give a soft dough. Cover and leave to rise for 5 minutes. Knead on a lightly floured surface, then press into a greased 1 lb (450 g) loaf tin. Cover with oiled polythene and leave in a warm place until the mixture reaches the top of the tin. Remove the polythene and bake in the oven at 200°C (400°F/Mark 6) for about 30 minutes. Cool on a wire tray. Serve sliced and buttered.

Makes 1 small loaf

Hot cross buns

These spicy buns are traditionally eaten on Good Friday, but if you leave the crosses off you can make them at any time

Barley flour 8 oz (225 g)
100% wholemeal flour 8 oz (225 g)
Ground cinnamon 2 tsp (10 ml)
Mixed spice 1½ tsp (7.5 ml)
Ground nutmeg 1 tsp (5 ml)
Salt 1 tsp (5 ml)
Fresh yeast 1 oz (25 g)
Water 4 tbsp (60 ml)
Raw brown sugar 2 oz (50 g)
Currants 4 oz (100 g)
Milk ¼ pt (142 ml)
Butter or margarine, melted 2 oz (50 g)
Free-range egg, beaten 1
Wholemeal shortcrust pastry (*see page 230*) 2 oz (50 g)

Glaze
Water 4 tbsp (60 ml)
Raw brown sugar 3 tbsp (45 ml)

Put the flours, spices and salt into a mixing bowl. Cream the yeast with the warm water and 1 tsp (5 ml) sugar and leave in a warm place until frothy. Combine the flour, yeast mixture, remaining sugar, currants, butter, egg and sufficient warm milk to give a soft, manageable dough. Divide the mixture into 12 pieces. Knead each one on a lightly floured surface and arrange them well apart on floured baking sheets. Leave in a warm place to prove until doubled in size. Roll out the pastry and cut into thin strips. Damp the strips and lay 2 on each bun to make a cross. Bake in the oven at 190°C (375°F/Mark 5) for about 20 minutes.

Glaze
Heat the water and sugar together. Bring to the boil. Brush over the buns twice, then leave to cool.

Makes 12 buns

Jam doughnuts

100% wholemeal flour 8 oz (225 g)
Salt ½ tsp (2.5 ml)
Oil 2 tbsp (30 ml)
Fresh yeast ½ oz (15 g)
Milk 4 tbsp (60 ml)
Free-range egg 1
Jam 10 tsp (50 ml)
Oil for frying
Raw brown sugar & cinnamon to coat

Put flour, salt and oil into a basin. Stir the yeast and warm milk together until smooth, then add to the flour with the egg. Mix to a soft dough. Cover and leave in a warm place to double in size (about ½ hour). Knead lightly, then divide into 10 pieces. Shape each into a round, put 1 tsp (5 ml) jam in the centre and shape the dough into a ball. Heat the oil and fry the doughnuts for about 5 minutes, until golden brown. Drain on absorbent paper. Sprinkle with sugar mixed with a little cinnamon. Serve warm, if possible.

Makes 10 doughnuts

Chelsea buns

A different way to make fruit buns

100% wholemeal flour 10 oz (300 g)
Fresh yeast ½ oz (15 g)
Milk 4 fl. oz (100 ml)
Salt ½ tsp (2.5 ml)
Margarine 1 oz (25 g)
Free-range egg, beaten 1
Butter or margarine, melted 2 oz (50 g)
Mixed dried fruits 4 oz (100 g)
Raw brown sugar 2 oz (50 g)
Honey to glaze

Grease a 11 × 7" (27 × 18 cm) cake tin. Put 2 oz (50 g) flour in a basin with the yeast and warm the milk. Beat until smooth.

Leave in a warm place until frothy. Meanwhile, put the remaining flour and salt in a basin. Rub in the margarine. Add the yeast mixture and beaten egg and mix to a soft dough. Knead on a lightly floured surface and then roll out to an oblong 15 × 12″ (38 × 30 cm). Brush with melted butter and sprinkle with dried fruit and sugar. Starting from a short side, roll up like a swiss roll. Cut into 12 pieces and arrange in the tin cut-side up. Leave to rise in a warm place, until the buns are touching and have risen to the top of the tin. Bake in the oven at 200°C (400°F/Mark 6) for 20–25 minutes. Brush with warmed honey and leave to cool in the tin.

Makes 12 buns

Pastry

The basic principles of cooking never change, but obviously recipes and results do, as the ingredients vary – and such is the case with pastry made with 100% wholemeal flour. The texture of shortcrust pastry is coarser than that made with refined white flour, and the absorption qualities of the wholemeal flour may vary a little, so that extra fat or liquid may be necessary to obtain a workable consistency. The flavour and texture of the wholemeal pastry is an altogether different experience to the characterless white product.

There are many people with preconceived ideas about the limitations of 100% wholemeal flour who will be surprised at the good results that can be obtained when it is used to make choux pastry. Success in the making of this pastry depends on the addition of water in the recipe to produce steam during the cooking process.

There are few lovelier sights in the culinary world than a deftly fashioned wholemeal pastry case for a flan or pie, with its decorated edge encompassed with absolute harmony in a stoneware dish thrown by a craftsman potter.

Wholemeal pastry chart – easy guide to quantities

100% wholemeal flour	Baking powder	Fat (Butter & Nutter in equal proportions)	Water (approx.)	Made weight of pastry (approx.)
100 g/4 oz	5 ml/1 tsp	50 g/2 oz	20 ml/4 tsp	175 g/6 oz
150 g/5 oz	7.5 ml/1½ tsp	75 g/2½ oz	30 ml/2 tbsp	225 g/8 oz
200 g/7 oz	10 ml/2 tsp	100 g/3½ oz	45 ml/3 tbsp	300 g/10 oz
250 g/9 oz	12.5 ml/2½ tsp	125 g/4½ oz	45–60 ml/ 3–4 tbsp	400 g/14 oz
300 g/10 oz	15 ml/1 tbsp	150 g/5 oz	45–60 ml/ 3–4 tbsp	450 g/1 lb
400 g/14 oz	20 ml/4 tsp	200 g/7 oz	60–75 ml/ 4–5 tbsp	600 g/1¼ lb

Wholemeal shortcrust pastry

This is the basic recipe to follow for shortcrust pastry when using brown flour

100% wholemeal flour 7 oz (200 g)
Baking powder 2 tsp (10 ml)
Butter or margarine 1¾ oz (50 g)
Nutter 1¾ oz (50 g)
Water 3 tbsp (45 ml)

Place flour and baking powder in a basin. Rub in the fats until the mixture resembles fine crumbs. Add sufficient water to give a soft but manageable dough.

VARIATION
Cheese pastry Add 4–6 oz (100–175 g) grated Cheddar cheese and ½ tsp (2.5 ml) mustard powder before the water is added.

Makes about 10 oz (300 g)

Hot water crust pastry

This pastry is easy to make and is particularly good for raised savoury pies. It has a firm texture when baked, unlike shortcrust pastry

100% wholemeal flour 1 lb (450 g)
Salt 2 tsp (10 ml)
White fat 4 oz (100 g)
Milk or milk & water ¼ pt + 2 tbsp (150 ml + 30 ml)

Put the flour and salt into a basin. Put the fat and liquid in a saucepan and heat until the fat is melted. Bring to the boil. Pour on to the flour and, with a wooden spoon, mix to form a soft dough. Cover with a damp teatowel or cling-wrap and leave to rest for ½ hour before using.

Makes about 1½ lb (675 g)

Choux pastry

Water ¼ pt (150 ml)
Butter or margarine 2 oz (50 g)
100% wholemeal flour 9 tbsp (135 ml)
Free-range eggs, beaten 2

Place the water and butter in a saucepan. Heat until the butter has melted, then bring to the boil. Off the heat, stir in the flour and beat with a wooden spoon until the mixture leaves the sides of the pan clean and forms a ball. Allow to cool slightly, then beat in the egg a little at a time, until thoroughly mixed.

Wholemeal pastry made with oil

An alternative type of shortcrust pastry, which may be a little more difficult to handle

100% wholemeal flour 8 oz (225 g)
Baking powder ½ tsp (2.5 ml)
Salt, pinch
Oil 5 tbsp (75 ml)
Cold water 3 tbsp (45 ml)

Put the flour, baking powder and salt in a basin. Whisk the oil and water together, then add to the dry ingredients. Work together to give a soft, manageable dough. Roll out on a lightly floured surface or between sheets of greaseproof paper.

Makes about 12 oz (350 g)

Preserves & Sweetmeats

Sugar is the indispensable ingredient in preserves because, quite simply, it is the preservative. Therefore if you are one of those who believe sugar in any form to be harmful to health, you should skip this chapter altogether, or use honey as an alternative (*see Bibliography on page 43*).

As mentioned in the introductory part of this book, we believe refined white sugar to be an unacceptable substance and we use, and recommend for use, only raw muscovado sugar which has had the minimum of treatment and retains the naturally occurring minerals and trace elements needed by the body. The molasses form of this sugar is very dark and would produce a very distinctive flavour. Some will like this, but the more generally useful form is the lighter variety which we find very good for all forms of cooking. Of course products made with this will have a different colour and flavour, but it is very unlikely that having experienced this quality you will want to return to a white sugar product.

Coarse-cut orange marmalade

A rich dark and full-flavoured marmalade

Seville oranges 3 lb (1.4 kg)
Lemon 1
Water 5¼ pt (3 l)
Pale raw brown sugar 5 lb (2.25 kg)

Wash the fruit and put it into a preserving pan with the water. Cover and simmer gently for about 2 hours, until the fruit is soft and the skins are easily pierced with a wooden skewer. Remove the fruit from the pan, reserve the cooking water. Cut the fruit in half and remove the pips. Put the pips in a pan with just enough of the reserved water to cover and simmer them while you cut up the peel. Slice the orange and lemon peel thickly and return it and the pulp to the preserving pan, with the strained liquid from the pips. Bring to the boil. Remove from the heat and stir in the sugar. Heat very gently, stirring frequently until the sugar dissolves. Bring to the boil, and boil for about 20 minutes, or until the marmalade jells

when tested on a plate. Pour into hot, sterilized jars and seal
with jam pot covers.

Makes about 8 lb (3.6 kg)

Lemon curd

Free-range eggs 2
Butter or margarine 4 oz (100 g)
Lemon, grated rind & juice of 2
Pale raw brown sugar 8 oz (225 g)

Beat the eggs and put all the ingredients into the top of a
double saucepan or in a basin standing in a pan of simmering
water. Stir until the sugar has dissolved and continue heating,
stirring from time to time until the curd thickens enough to
coat the back of a wooden spoon. Pour into hot, sterilized jars
and seal with jam pot covers.

VARIATION
Orange curd Substitute oranges for lemons, and add juice of ½
lemon.

Makes 1 lb (450 g)

Apple butter

*In spite of its misleading name, this preserve is really a thick, firm
apple jam*

Cooking apples 3 lb (1.4 kg)
Water 1¾ pt (1 l)
Pale raw brown sugar, about 3 lb (1.4 kg)
Ground cinnamon (optional) ½ tsp (2.5 ml)
Ground cloves (optional) ½ tsp (2.5 ml)

Wash and chop the apples without peeling or removing the
cores. Cover with water and simmer gently until pulpy. Sieve
and weigh the pulp, then return it to the pan. Add ¾ lb (350
g) sugar for every 1 lb (450 g) apple pulp. Add spices, if
wished. Heat gently, stirring occasionally until the sugar is

dissolved, then boil until thick and creamy in consistency. Pour into hot, sterilized jars and seal with jam pot covers.

Makes 6 lb (2.8 kg)

Apple & ginger chutney

This country recipe, which is ideal for using up windfall apples, is given a piquant flavour by the ginger, garlic and pickling spice

Cider vinegar 1¼ pt (750 ml)
Raw brown sugar 1½ lb (675 g)
Pickling spice ½ oz (15 g)
Cooking apples 2¼ lb (1 kg)
Onions 8 oz (225 g)
Root ginger 4 oz (100 g)
Garlic cloves 1 oz (25 g)
Salt 1 oz (25 g)
Sultanas 4 oz (100 g)

Heat the vinegar and sugar slowly in a large saucepan until the sugar is dissolved. Meanwhile, tie the pickling spice in a small piece of muslin. Core and chop the apples, skin and chop the onion, peel and grate the root ginger and peel and crush the garlic. Add all the ingredients to the pan, bring to the boil, reduce heat and simmer, stirring occasionally, for about 2 hours, or until the mixture is thick and no 'free' liquid remains. Remove the pickling spice. Pour the chutney into hot, sterilized jars and cover with vinegar-proof paper.

Makes about 4 lb (2 kg)

Fruit & nut chews

These sweets are quick and easy to make as there is no sugar-boiling involved

Raisins 4 oz (100 g)
Stoned dates 4 oz (100 g)
Walnuts 4 oz (100 g)
Desiccated coconut 2 oz (50 g)

Using a mincer fitted with a coarse blade, mince the raisins, dates and walnuts together. Add the coconut and work the mixture with the fingertips until it binds. Form into thin rolls and cut into bite-size pieces.

Makes about 24

Marzipan shapes

Marzipan (*see page 178*) 8 oz (225 g)
Walnut halves 12
Fresh dates 12

Walnut Rounds
Roll half the marzipan into 12 balls. Press a walnut half on to each.

Date Barrels
Remove the stones from the dates. Shape the remaining marzipan into 12 'barrel' shapes and press into the middle of each date.

Makes 24

Coconut bars

This wholefood adaptation of coconut ice will keep in the refrigerator for about one week

Cream cheese 3 oz (75 g)
Raw brown sugar 2 oz (50 g)
Desiccated coconut 4 oz (100 g)
Mixed nuts, finely ground 2 oz (50 g)

Work all the ingredients together until evenly mixed. Shape into a bar, then cut into pieces. Leave on greaseproof paper to 'dry'.

Makes about 20 bars

Carob 'fudge'

A soft textured sweet, rather like fudge

Butter or margarine 2 oz (50 g)
Carob powder 1 oz (25 g)
Clear honey 2 oz (50 g)
Soya flour 1 oz (25 g)
Ground almonds 3 oz (75 g)
Vanilla essence (1 tsp) (5 ml)
Almonds, ground or finely chopped 1 oz (25 g)

Cream the butter and carob powder until well mixed. Add the
next 4 ingredients and mix thoroughly. Sprinkle the ground
almonds on a clean dry working surface and shape the 'fudge'
into a roll, coating it with the almonds. Cut into bite-size
pieces. Keep in the refrigerator until required.

VARIATION
Sesame 'fudge' Replace 1 oz (25 g) ground almonds with 1 oz
(25 g) toasted sesame seeds.

Dried apricot & almond jam

*A delicious whole fruit jam that can be made at any time of the
year. The whole almonds may be omitted if wished*

Dried apricots 1 lb (450 g)
Lemon, juice of 1
Pale raw brown sugar 3 lb (1.4 kg)
Whole almonds, blanched 3 oz (75 g)

Wash the apricots, then cover with 3 pt (1.7 l) water and leave
to soak for 24 hours. Put the fruit with the water and lemon
juice in a large saucepan or preserving pan and simmer for ½
hour. Add the sugar, and almonds if wished, and stir over
gentle heat until the sugar is dissolved. Bring to the boil and
boil rapidly, stirring frequently, until the jam jells when tested
on a plate. Pour into hot, sterilized jars and cover with jam pot
covers. Cool and store.

Makes about 5 lb (2.3 kg)

Drinks

One tends to overlook the fact that a drink is often more than just liquid and can really be a liquid food, and as such can be at least as nourishing as solid food. In fact it is possible to get a considerably bigger intake of vitamins and minerals from raw fruit and vegetables by drinking the extracted juices than by trying to munch through them in their solid state. But it is important to remember to drink these juices slowly (preferably through a straw) because of the concentration of the food and the time needed to digest it.

In the Bircher-Benner Sanatorium in Zurich, Switzerland, they specialize in the treatment of degenerative diseases with the use of raw foods and juices and achieve many wonderful results, even with cases labelled incurable by the medical profession. They say that raw juices are the Life Blood of the vegetables, containing the vital enzymes and digestive factors so important for keeping our bodies in a healthy condition.

We introduced raw juices on our menu from the time we first opened Cranks in 1961, producing them laboriously in domestic juice extractors, and even to this day with a vastly bigger business we still have to use these small-scale juicers. A juice extractor should not be confused with a liquidizer. The extractor operates by forcing root vegetables or hard fruit down on to a very high revolution grater plate which has the effect of throwing the juices to the outer circumference by centrifugal force through a sieve and then out of the machine through a spout. The residual roughage is either collected and occasionally emptied or is ejected during the operation. A liquidizer or blender, on the other hand, is a goblet at the bottom of which are fast rotating and cutting blades. Chopped fruit or vegetables are dropped into a liquid (water, stock or juice) and are chopped up very finely by the blades and blended evenly with the liquid until they have a smooth creamy consistency.

The flavour of the extracted juices defies description – they seem to radiate a pure life force which puts them on another plane from other foods. Many other healthy and flavoursome drinks, of course, such as yeast-based drinks, herb teas and others, are good alternatives to coffee, chocolate and malted drinks, which are often harmful to health. The chart below should assist those who are starting out on the adventure of changing to a health food regime.

Some drinks which are commonly consumed can be harmful to health when drunk on a regular basis. Tea and coffee are stimulants and can be damaging to the nervous and digestive systems. We have set out below some alternatives as a guide for those wishing to change to a more healthy intake.

INSTEAD OF	DRINK
Fresh or instant coffee	Dandelion coffee Decaffeinated coffee Cereal grain coffee
Tea	Matte tea, possibly with just a pinch of your favourite tea Fresh herb or tisane teas
Wine	Aspall apple juice (organic) Grape juice *Ideal for drinking and driving*
Tap water (mostly recycled many times, and often fluorinated)	Bottled mineral water, e.g. Vichy, Perrier, Ashbourne
Bottled squashes	Lane's blackcurrant juice or rosehip juice (unsweetened) – dilute with mineral water
Bovril	Vecon (a seaweed drink) Barmene or Tastex (yeast drinks)
Malted milk	Emprote (a high-protein drink)
Cocoa and drinking chocolate	Honey cup (carob drink) Barley cup or Kabafit

Freshly extracted vegetable & fruit juices

Freshly extracted juices have always been a speciality in Cranks since its opening in 1961, and Cranks is often asked 'How do we make them at home, does it take long, is it worth the trouble?' The answer to the last question is definitely 'Yes'. The reward of exciting flavours and absolutely 'instant vitamins' ensures that all the drinks are worth the trouble. Whether they are served on their own or mixed with other ingredients, there is a wide range of flavours.

Although juicing is a fairly time-consuming process, the preparation of the raw ingredients is simple, and with the help of an electric juice separator you can have freshly extracted juices without much effort. While compiling this book, Cranks tested the Kenwood Juice Separator and found it really efficient, reasonably priced, and fairly easy to assemble and clean. It is used for extracting the juice from vegetables and fruits, other than citrus fruit. The Kenwood Juice Extractor attachment is useful for making orange, grapefruit and lemon juice, particularly if it is required in large quantities. The alternative method of preparation is to use a hand-squeezer.

Extracted juices are very concentrated and should be taken in moderation – Gaylord Hauser recommends 1 pt (600 ml) of juice a day! To give you an idea of amounts of 'raw materials' required:

> *1 lb (450 g) carrots produces 1/3 pt (200 ml) juice*
> *1 lb (450 g) apples produces 1/3 pt (200 ml) juice*
> *1 lb (450 g) tomatoes produces 1/2 pt (300 ml) juice*
> *1 lb (450 g) blackberries produces 1/2 pt (300 ml) juice*

There are many excellent books on the subject of 'juicing' and these are referred to in the Bibliography (*see page 43*).

Bottled juices

A range of good quality bottled fruit juices is available from most health food shops. Particular favourites of Cranks are

Aspall Hall apple juice and cider. The apple juice is made from thirty-three varieties of apples, organically grown in the grounds of Aspall Hall in Suffolk – with no added chemicals or preservatives. The juice extracted from these apples is either bottled as juice or allowed to ferment naturally. Fermentation is slow and it is two years before the cider is mature and ready for bottling. Lane's blackcurrant and rosehip juices are particularly good for children as a vitamin C supplement, and they contain only raw sugar and no preservatives or colouring.

Preparation for extracted juices

Watercress juice. A dark green juice, best used in combination with other juices. Wash watercress leaves and stalks in a colander. Feed through the extractor in small bunches, adding a little water to aid the extraction.

Spinach juice. A dark green juice, very concentrated and best used with other juices or whisked up with yoghourt and a pinch of Biosalt. Wash leaves and stalks well and feed small handfuls through the extractor with a little water.

Parsley & mint juice. Another dark green juice which should be combined with carrot or tomato – the method is as for spinach.

Cabbage juice. Strongly flavoured but good combined with other juices. It is best to use young green cabbage. Wash well and roughly chop. Feed through the extractor with a little water.

Carrot juice. This juice has a wonderful flavour and colour and mixes well with other juices. Wash carrots well but do not peel or top and tail. Cut into convenient chunks to fit the extractor. Add a little lemon juice after juicing as this helps to keep its colour and prevents it going brown.

Celery juice. This juice is best used mixed with another juice as it is quite strong. Add a little lemon juice to prevent discoloration and store away from bright light. Wash celery, including leaves, and cut into convenient lengths.

Cucumber juice. In spite of a bland flavour, one cucumber will yield a lot of juice compared with other vegetables. Wash cucumber and cut up. It is delicious blended with a little lemon juice and honey.

Apple juice. This makes a very tasty drink and combines well with most of the vegetable juices. Always add lemon juice to prevent discoloration. Wash and cut up apples but do not peel or core. Remove any imperfections.

Tomato juice. A lovely drink which tastes so different from tinned tomato juice. Wash and chop tomatoes. It combines well with yoghourt, and a pinch of Biosalt improves the flavour.

Pineapple juice. Peel and cut up into convenient pieces to fit the extractor. Makes a delicious juice for drinks and fruit salad syrup.

Grape juice. A tasty drink and a juice which combines well with other juices. Wash grapes and feed through the extractor. It also makes a good base for fruit salads.

Soft fruit juices. Pick over the fruits and push through a sieve or feed through the juice extractor. It is sometimes necessary to pour a little water through at the same time.

Keep all extracted juices in the refrigerator and cover.

Recipes for drinks as served in Cranks

Carrot, apple (or orange) & honey. Measure 1 part apple (or orange) juice and 4 parts carrot juice into a liquidizer goblet. Add honey to taste and blend for a few seconds.

Mixed vegetable. Measure 2 parts carrot juice and 1 part each of celery and cucumber juice into a liquidizer goblet. Blend for a few seconds.

Carrot & spinach (or watercress). Measure 3 parts carrot juice and 1 part spinach (or watercress) juice into a liquidizer goblet. Blend for a few seconds.

Apple & cabbage. Measure 3 parts apple juice and 1 part cabbage juice into a liquidizer goblet. Blend for a few seconds.

Cucumber, lemon & honey. Measure 3 parts cucumber juice and 1 part lemon juice into a liquidizer goblet. Add honey to sweeten and blend for a few seconds.

Watercress, tomato & apple. Measure 1 part each of watercress juice and tomato juice and 2 parts apple juice into a liquidizer goblet. Blend for a few seconds.

Lemon (or orange) fizz. Wash and chop ½ lemon (or orange) and place in a liquidizer goblet. Pour on sufficient water to cover and blend until smooth. Strain through a fine nylon sieve into a glass, or jug, and top up with Perrier water. Sweeten to taste with honey, if wished.

Yoghourt, milk & honey. Put ¼ pt (142 ml) each fresh milk and natural yoghourt in a liquidizer goblet. Add 1–2 tsp (5–10 ml) honey and blend until smooth. Serve chilled.

Juice, yoghourt & milk drink. The juice may be freshly extracted or the bottled kind. Use any flavour you like. Salt can be added to savoury drinks. A little honey or raw brown sugar can be added to sweet drinks. Put 4 fl. oz (100 ml) fruit or vegetable juice and 3 fl. oz (75 ml) each fresh milk and natural yoghourt in a liquidizer goblet. Blend until smooth. Serve chilled.

Tiger's milk. This is a Gaylord Hauser recipe. Put ¼ pt (150 ml) each fresh milk and orange juice in a liquidizer goblet.

Add 2 tsp (10 ml) skimmed milk powder and 1 tsp (5 ml) each Brewer's yeast and molasses. Blend until smooth and serve chilled.

Banana milk. Put a peeled ripe banana and ½ pt (284 ml) fresh milk in a liquidizer goblet. Blend until smooth. Serve chilled.

Curvacious cocktail. This is a Gaylord Hauser recipe. Put ⅓ pt (200 ml) fresh orange juice, 1 free-range egg, 1 tbsp (15 ml) wheatgerm and 1 tsp (5 ml) honey in a liquidizer goblet. Blend until smooth and serve chilled.

Yoghourt, milk & fruit drink. Put 4 oz (100 g) fresh fruit (raspberries, strawberries, stoned apricots, etc.), ¼ pt (142 ml) yoghourt and ½ pt (284 ml) milk into a liquidizer goblet. Add raw brown sugar or honey to taste and blend until smooth. Sieve, if wished, before serving.

Cranks home-made lemonade

This lovely drink is made every day in Cranks using fresh lemons and raw sugar. Occasionally when the sugar is extra dark it is nick-named 'Thames Mud' and some of our foreign customers wonder what on earth it is! The sharp, fresh flavour bears absolutely no relationship to the present-day bottled variety found in the supermarket – how could a simple drink like this have deteriorated so much?

It is definitely well worth the effort to buy extra lemons and make this at home. The recipe suggests raw sugar, but is quite possible to use honey instead, and some people, particularly children, might prefer this. The strength of lemons varies considerably and it may be advisable to dilute the lemonade, particularly for children who may not have experienced the flavour of real lemons and could be put off if it is served too strong.

Lemons 4
Raw brown sugar 6 oz (175 g)
Boiling water 1½ pt (900 ml)

Scrub the lemons, halve them, then squeeze out the juice. Place the juice and pulp in a large jug or bowl with the sugar and pour ½ pt (300 ml) boiling water over. Stir until the sugar dissolves. Add the lemon halves and another 1 pt (600 ml) boiling water. Stir well, then cover and leave to cool. Strain, squeezing out the juice from the lemon halves and serve.

Makes about 1½ pt (900 ml)

Lemon brose

This is a real 'old-fashioned' drink, based on oatmeal, that is easy to make, nutritious and satisfying – and is especially suitable for children.

Oatmeal, medium 2 oz (50 g)
Raw brown sugar 1 tbsp (15 ml)
Lemon 1
Water ½ pt (300 ml)

Put the oatmeal in a jug with the raw brown sugar. Squeeze the juice from the lemon and add to the oatmeal together with the lemon halves. Pour ½ pt (300 ml) boiling water over and stir well. Cover and leave to cool. Strain, squeezing out the juice from the lemon halves, thin to the required consistency with water, and serve.

VARIATION
Orange Brose Substitute 1 orange for 1 lemon.

If wished, this drink may be served warm. A tot of whisky gives a 'kick'! The same recipe can be used for Lemon or Orange Barley Drink – use barley flakes instead of the oatmeal.

Herb tea or tisane

Many people grow herbs in their garden and use them for cooking, but few use them for making drinks. Herb teas are considered to be beneficial to the body, each herb having specific qualities.

For fresh herb teas, pick a large sprig of mint, lemon balm or other fresh herb, wash it carefully, then place it in a small jug, and pour on boiling water. Leave to infuse for up to 5 minutes, then strain into a cup. It is sometimes possible to buy a glass teapot for making herb teas – with this you can see the infusion as well as taste it.

There is, of course, a great variety of herb tea sachets sold in health food shops – rosehip, camomile, lime flower, peppermint and many others – and these, apart from being very convenient to use, make a most acceptable substitute for coffee or tea. Simple place one sachet in a cup or small jug, and pour on boiling water. Leave for a few minutes, remove the sachet and then drink – sweeten with a little honey if desired.

Hot drinks

Carob milk. Mix 2–3 tsp (10–15 ml) carob powder with a little cold milk measured from ½ pt (284 ml) until there is a smooth paste. Heat the remaining milk and pour over the carob paste, stirring. Sweeten if wished.

This drink can also be served chilled.

Honey & lemon. Put 1 tsp (5 ml) honey, 1 tbsp (15 ml) lemon juice and a slice of lemon in a glass. Place a metal spoon in the glass then pour in ¼ pt (150 ml) boiling water. Stir and serve. If wished a tot of whisky or rum can be added.

VARIATION
Use a small orange instead of lemon.

Dandelion root 'coffee'. For each cup: Put 1 tsp (5 ml) dandelion root in a saucepan with ½ pt (200 ml) water. Bring to the boil, reduce heat and simmer for 10 minutes. Strain, and serve as coffee, with or without milk.

Honegar. Put 1 tsp (5 ml) each cider vinegar and honey into a glass. Place a metal spoon in the glass and stir in ¼ pt (150 ml) hot water until the honey dissolves.

Clear mineral broth – makes about 1½ pt (900 ml). Prepare and roughly chop a celery heart, one large onion, 2 oz (50 g) spinach, 2 sticks celery and 2 medium-sized carrots. Place in a saucepan with 1½ pt (900 ml) water, 1 tsp (5 ml) salt and a few parsley sprigs. Cover and simmer for about 30 minutes, then strain. Serve at once. The broth may be covered and refrigerated and reheated as required.

Index

For general cookery information, see under *Culinary know-how*.